The Scottish Lochs 2

Constable London

The Scottish Lochs 2
Tom Weir

Published by
Constable & Company Ltd
10 Orange Street   London WC2

© Copyright 1972 Tom Weir
First published 1972
Set in 'Monotype' Baskerville

Printed in England by
W & J Mackay Limited
Chatham

Photographs by the author

Books by the same author
Highland Days
The Ultimate Mountains
Camps and Climbs in Arctic Norway
East of Katmandu
Focus on Mountains
The Scottish Lochs 1

The author would like to acknowledge the help
given by the officers of the Nature Conservancy
in Scotland.

overleaf: Loch Maree and the Peak of Slioch

Contents

Stornoway

Langavat

Lumain

Shell
Fionn
Maree

Scadavay

Benbecula
Bee
Druidibeg

Storr

Coruisk

Scale: 12 miles to 1 inch

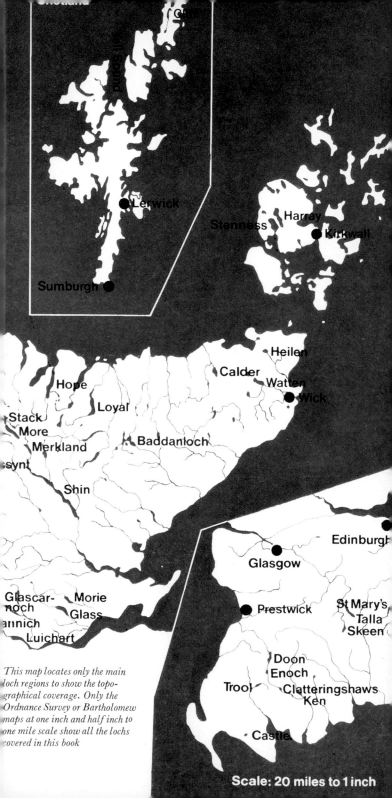

Scotland

Shetland Isles

Lerwick

Sumburgh

Stenness

Harray

Kirkwall

Heilen

Calder

Watten

Wick

Hope

Loyal

Stack

More

Merkland

ssynt

Shin

Baddanloch

Edinburgh

Glasgow

Prestwick

St Mary's
Talla
Skeen

Glascar-
noch

annich

Morie

Glass

Luichart

Doon

Enoch

Trool

Clatteringshaws

Ken

Castle

*This map locates only the main
loch regions to show the topo-
graphical coverage. Only the
Ordnance Survey or Bartholomew
maps at one inch and half inch to
one mile scale show all the lochs
covered in this book*

Scale: 20 miles to 1 inch

Introduction

This volume of the Scottish lochs deals with north and
south Scotland and complements Volume 1 which
takes in all the country from Loch Lomond to the
Beauly Firth, from the Atlantic coast to the North Sea.
Volume 2 sweeps on northward to Cape Wrath and
east to John o' Groats, crossing over the Pentland
Firth to Orkney and Shetland, west to the Outer
Hebrides, then far south to the Galloway Highlands
and the Borders, in the drainage basins of Clyde,
Solway and Tweed.

Much of this north and south country of Scotland
is still remote. In the Uists for example, where the
trout, sea-trout and salmon fishing has the quality of
legend, there are half a dozen lochs unfished for every
one fished. Fair Isle and Shetland are a crossroads for
arctic bird migrants, but strange things have been
happening here of recent years. The snowy owl has
become a nester, redwings have established colonies
in the woods of Ross, Sutherland and Inverness-shire,
the wood sandpiper has become established in wet
floes, the bluethroat has nested and a brood of great
northern divers has been reared.

The wanderer in the lonely north country will find
himself surrounded by echoes of the past. On an island
on a loch he may see a stone fortification, an ancient
'dun' with an underwater causeway leading to it. On
the shore there may be a stone circle or a megalithic
burial tomb. This is the country of the 'brochs',
mysterious round towers which occur only here in the
world. Archaeologists still puzzle over who built them.
Their latest findings are described in this book.

In country where there are distinctive valleys, as in
most of the mainland dealt with, it has been easy to
arrange the lochs by their drainage basins, but in peat
blanket covering Lewisian gneiss where the lochs are
mere hollows and connections hard to trace, this
system breaks down, especially when many of the
lochs have no name. So in the lochscape of Sutherland
and the Outer Islands I have chosen representative
samples to give a picture of the whole.

From the Highlands and Islands to the Lowlands
seems a big jump, but the decision to include Galloway
and the Borders with the north and west was made
with the convenience of users in mind. Volume 1
covers the Highland area most visited by tourists.

Volume 2 in the main gets more off the beaten track, and much of Galloway is as unknown as Caithness to tourists.

It is the author's hope that readers will be attracted by the new motorways to explore the south-west and the Borders. High Galloway is in fact a miniature of the Cairngorms. The rock is granite, and though the scale is only half that of the Grampian massif, the atmosphere is the same when you get up among the lonelier lochs where the rounded boulders look like curling stones on the ice-scored slabs round the shores of Loch Enoch under Craignaw. The best of it can only be reached on foot, which is all to the good.

Although these two volumes on the Scottish Lochs purport to deal only with freshwaters, this definition has been stretched a little in the Outer Hebrides and North Isles where some lochs are marginally salt because of the tide spilling in from time to time. No loch has been described which does not support a freshwater fauna, which I think is a fair criterion.

Gartocharn
August 1971

The summit of Slioch above Loch Maree

Lochs of the Ewe Basin

Lochs Maree, Tollaidh, Fada, Clair, Coulin, Kernsary,
Ghiuragarstidh, a' Bhaid Luachriach, Mhic Ille Riabhaich,
nan Dailthean, an t' Slagain, Sguod, an Drainc

It is almost a cliché to compare Loch Lomond and
Loch Maree. But the 'Bonny Banks' would not be
right for the Ross-shire loch. It does not have that
kind of sylvan charm. The slopes are altogether
steeper, rockier, wetter, more heathery. Loch Maree
is more the embodiment of what is called 'Highland
grandeur', a rough description appropriate to such a
shaggy tumble of crag and water.

It is the largest loch north of the Great Glen but has
less than half the area of Loch Lomond, 11·03 sq.
miles as against the 27·45 for Scotland's biggest loch,
and defeats it on only one measurement. Loch Maree
has a bigger proportionate area of islands to water
surface than Loch Lomond. This is known as the
insulosity factor, which is 0·09 as against 0·08. But
Loch Maree has recently acquired a more unique
distinction. It is now the largest entirely natural loch
remaining in Scotland, Loch Lomond having been
reduced to the status of reservoir and Loch Ness and
Loch Awe harnessed for hydro-electric pumping
stations.

The immediate similarity between Loch Lomond
and Loch Maree is one of impact. You are presented
with the whole rather than the part. The aura is
immediate. You respond to it as to music. But whereas
Loch Lomond is Mozart, Loch Maree is Beethoven,
more sombre, more profound, casting you more back
into yourself. On Loch Maree you have the feeling of
a primeval landscape.

The very woods above you on Ben Eighe are fragments of the Caledonian pine forest dating back 8,000
years. Across the loch on Slioch the bare bones of the
peak thrust up to a summit, with more strength and
force than Ben Lomond. The colours are sombre, dun
rather than emerald. The rocks swell out of the ground
in grey bosses, ice-scored and polished, changing
colour to pink where the layers of Torridonian sandstone have been heaved over the grey gneiss as on
Slioch. Here it is no surprise to meet a wild cat, an
otter, red and roe deer, or a pine marten. Eagle and

The deepest part of Loch Maree is under Slioch

peregrine falcon can appear in the sky any time. Man has not made much impact here yet.

However, there were iron-works here 350 years ago, consuming 20 acres of oaks daily for charcoal until 'the woods of it were all spent up and the lease expired'. That quotation came from Letterewe on the roadless shore of the loch, but it could have applied to Fasagh, Poolewe or Talladale, where there were other 'bloomeries', using bog-iron and charcoal from the oakwoods to make pig-iron for cannons, among other things.

The remains of the bloomery at Furnace can still be seen on Loch Maree. The charcoal from the burned woods was taken to the bloomery which was in two storeys, the charcoal and iron-ore being dropped from above into the closed furnace, then a set of bellows below would blow the fuel to the heat required to melt the iron from the slag. At five tons of timber to smelt one ton of pig-iron it was expensive in raw material, but the demand for iron was high, and it was met so long as the supply of oaks lasted.

All the more miraculous then that so much oak and pine forest should remain, especially when timber shortages in the last two wars made inroads on Coille na Glas Leitire – 'Wood of the Grey Slope', which has been growing here for 8,000 years and since 1951 has been the object of intensive study by Nature Conservancy scientists trying to encourage and regenerate it. Beinn Eighe, appropriately enough, became Britain's first National Nature Reserve when the Conservancy was formed.

So the perfect way to begin exploring Loch Maree is to pay a visit to the Information Centre at the Field Station of Anancaun, talk to the Warden, and set out armed with a pamphlet on the Nature Trail which rises from the lochside picnic site about three miles north of Kinlochewe. Short-stay campers are allowed to put their tents down at Taagan, where the loch begins, and it is a convenient place on good grass with no charge for its use.

The farm lands between here and Kinlochewe are on alluvium built up by river action in a silting process that has pushed steadily forward thus shrinking gradually the size of Loch Maree. The rivers have a powerful flow here and can raise the loch nine feet when the rainfall is high. Six inches fell in 24 hours on one March day of 1968 bringing down a great deal of

Pine marten in Ben Eighe nature reserve

Loch Maree – red deer hind and calf

debris. Small wonder that the large alluvial cones on some of the streams where they enter the loch are more marked on Loch Maree than on the majority of lochs. Conversely, low water can cause separate islands to join up with each other.

Why the name Kinlochewe for a village removed fifteen miles from the sea loch of that name? The explanation seems to be that Loch Ewe was the old name of Loch Maree before Saint Maelrubha came to Eilean Maruighe in the seventh century and made the small island famous as a place of pilgrimage. So Maruighe became the name of the loch and was corrupted to Maree, which is the English form for the 12-mile loch aligned along a major fault. Murray and Pullar in the *Bathymetrical Survey of the Scottish Freshwater Lochs* made the length $13\frac{1}{2}$ miles by taking in part of the so-called River Ewe, which they say more properly belongs to the loch because soundings of 30 ft were obtained.

It was Charles Darwin who said that every journey is made worthwhile if you pursue some kind of study on it. The chance to put this wise precept into action should not be missed on Loch Maree where the Nature Conservancy has made it easy for the tourist to see beyond the scenery. Armed with your pamphlet the circular Nature Trail takes only an hour, or you can turn it into a mountain walk that takes four hours.

The junction of the ways is a fine viewpoint at 350 ft crowned by a log cabin. Now you can look over the pink-barked pines to Slioch rising hugely above the deepest part of the loch where the bed digs down to 336 ft. Slioch – 'The Spear' – is a pyramid of warm sandstone thrust on top of grey bosses of Lewisian gneiss whose lower gullies hang with oaks and birch, multi-coloured in autumn.

A geological plinth constructed like layers of a cake shows the succession of the rocks, enabling you to detect how the peaks are built up. That lower grey of Slioch is Lewisian gneiss – the very floor of the world whose age goes back some 2,000 million years and more. The darker Torridonian sandstone on top is only half as old, but is one of the most ancient of rocks, formed under the sea or exposed as desert before it was squeezed up and pushed over the older surface. The sparkling white rocks capping the tops is Cambrian

Ben Eighe nature trail, Loch Maree

quartzite, the only one of the three to have fossilised remains of life in it. Examine it in the plinth and you can see the tubular worm casts of the earliest organisms. The world was entirely lifeless when the gneiss and the sandstone were formed.

Knowing these facts it is easy to detect the shapes of the older land surface under the sandstone. At the time of maximum glaciation, before Loch Maree was formed, the ice-cap covered the entire landscape, including the top of Slioch. The glaciers grinding and scraping in various directions at different times, sliced out valleys like Glen Torridon and exploited weaknesses like the Loch Maree fault.

Loch Maree occupies the greatest of the west-north-west group of faults—weaknesses in the Earth's crust where great slipping movements have altered the lay of the rocks horizontally and vertically. The wooded islands of the loch are composed of Torridonian sandstone and grits, though the nearby shore rocks on the north-east are Lewisian gneiss rising to heights of 2,000 ft. Climb Slioch and you will find boulders of the oldest rock have been carried on ice as high as the Cambrian quartzite near the top of the peak—all part of the history of formation and glaciation.

As with Loch Lomond the score of islands are situated in a group, many of them covered in natural woodland. One of them—the largest—Eilean Subhainn, even has its own loch with little islands on it. The size of the island is only 292 acres but the loch is 250 yds by 70 yds, and the maximum depth goes down to 64 ft. As with Isle Maree, Eilean Grudididh and Eilean Ruarid Bheag there is evidence of former habitation.

Isle Maree is the most famous island of any loch in Scotland, and much has been written about its sacred and Druidical associations. What St Columba did for Iona, St Maelrubha did for Isle Maree by setting up his cell here. Isle Maree was invested with special holy properties, well described by Thomas Pennant when he paid his visit in 1772 and wrote thus:

'Land on Inch-Maree, the favoured isle of the saint, the patron of all the coast from Applecross to Lochbroom. . . . The curiosity of the place is the well of the saint; of power unspeakable in cases of lunacy. The patient is brought to the sacred island, is made to kneel before the altar, where his attendants leave an offering in money; he is then brought to the well, and sips some of the holy water: a second offering is made;

that done he is thrice dipped in the lake. The same
operation is repeated every day for some weeks: and
it often happens, by natural causes, the patient receives
relief of which the saint receives credit.'

Queen Victoria came to it in 1877, at a time when
mentally ill people were still being brought to the
well, though most went just to wish a wish and hammer
a coin edgeways into the bark of the 'Wishing Tree',
or nail a scrap of clothing to the old oak, which died
under such treatment. The oaks of the Druids and the
holly of the Christians still flourish side by side,
but the Holy Well has been filled in. Today there
remains only the stones, and the burial ground among
the trees. No steamer runs on the loch now, nor is
there any ferry service between north and south
shore. The only hope of visiting the island is to try for
a boat at Loch Maree Hotel. My own visit was made
in March on a stormy day of white horses on the
water, but the island was in a sheltered oasis of calm –
peaceful as a church.

From Isle Maree south-west to the head of the loch
is known as the Grudie Basin, the deepest of the three
basins into which the loch is subdivided, with the
greatest depth of 367 ft where the loch is most
constricted between Slioch and Meall Ghuibhais –
'The Hill of the Firs' – now spanned by Nature and
Mountain Trails. In this basin the 200-ft depth extends
for over six miles, deepening to 300 ft for two miles,
and to 350 ft for one mile.

The Slattadale Basin is the island area, from west of
Eilean Ruaridh Mor to south of Eilean Subhainn,
where the 150-ft area has a depth of 2 miles by a
$\frac{1}{4}$ of a mile. Deep channels extend round the islands
and the 200-ft area stretches $1\frac{1}{2}$ miles by 150 yards
broad south of Eilean Ruaridh, the greatest depth of
232 ft being in the north-west.

The Ardlair Basin is more irregular than the other
two with a maximum depth of 285 ft where the floor
of the loch is bumpy with small hills. But the 200-ft
area runs for $2\frac{1}{2}$ miles and averages $\frac{1}{4}$ of a mile in
breadth. North of the islands there is a remarkable
shallowing to less than fifty feet. South of Isle Maree
there is also a large sandflat covered by no more than
a foot of water in times of low rainfall.

The salmon and sea-trout are the pride of Loch
Maree, and the hotel at Talladale is one of the most
reputable fishing inns in Scotland, spring time for the

The Geological Plinth, Ben Eighe nature trail, Loch Maree

salmon, summer to autumn for the big sea-trout which run up to 20 lbs. The mail bus carries passengers up this west side of Loch Maree, but 120 years ago when there was no road, all the letters from Gairloch parish, plus those from Lewis and Harris, were carried in the leather bag of Iain Mor am Posda – Big John the Post. Correspondence must have been light in those days when Big John tramped to and from Dingwall with his bag.

The route he followed was the drove road on the other side of the loch and the track is a Right of Way, curling through oak and birch woods, climbing over rocky passes, then dropping again with constantly changing vistas as the ridges and tops of Ben Eighe and Liathach spike into view, powdered as if with snow, the quartzite emphasising the verticality of the great drops plunging downward in wall upon wall of precipice. Lots of wild goats on this side, superbly horned and hairy. Letterewe, the shooting lodge,

Aid to spoor, Ben Eighe nature trail

stands in an oasis of lawns and gardens, at a cross-
roads of paths leading into the wildest hinterland in
Scotland, to the Fionn Loch, to Lochan Fada and
Loch na Sealga which I shall deal with later.

Visitors are not encouraged here, but cannot be
prevented from using the paths. However, a fine walk
has been opened up on the other bit of roadless shore
where the public highway swings away from the loch
at Slattadale, but a footpath goes on to Tollie following through woods and climbing over a pass to a little
peak called Creag Mhor Thollaidh less than 400 ft
above the highest point of the path. This is a thrilling
viewpoint, not only for the loch and its islands, but for
Skye and the Hebrides and the monolithic peaks of
Sutherland.

The Mountain Trail at the other end of the loch is
slightly more strenuous. It was opened in 1970 after
relays of voluntary workers had dug, drained, carried
stones and built bridges over some of the most difficult

Loch Maree, east shore where there are no roads, only tracks

rock and heather in the neighbourhood. Naval
helicopters carried material and the Royal Highland
Fusiliers helped load and unload it, a big combined
operation resulting in perhaps the finest hill path to be
built this century. It climbs to a Conservation Cairn
and Indicator Viewpoint at 1,800 ft.

It begins at the highest point of the Nature Trail,
following up the line of the Allt an Airidhe gorge
where the trees gradually thin out as they become
gnarled and dwarfed by wind. Green patches of good
grass and flowers show where the soil is lime-rich. The
demarcation is clear as long heather gives way to a
sward of grasses dotted with globe flowers, chickweed
wintergreen, moonwort, etc. High above the cleft of
the gorge there is a more startling change of scene, as
you climb out to a plateau of quartzite cradling little
saucer lochs. It has been well named a lunarscape.

A line of cairns makes route finding easy. Arctic
plants grow in the thin soil. Prostrate junipers, Alpine
bearberry, mountain azaleas are only a few of the

Conservation Corps Volunteers building a mountain trail

plants on this contrasty soil and vegetation. Scientific
exploration since 1951 has revealed that the flora is
richer than was suspected when Beinn Eighe became
Britain's first Nature Reserve.

Good work has been done too on the biology of the
pine marten whose stronghold is here amongst the old
trees. Extremely secretive and nocturnal in its habits,
it took Warden Dick Balharry three years to find a den.
He got his first in 1967, and told me something about
that encounter. He had managed to grab a young one
when it came to the mouth of the hole, and was
pulling it out by the tail when something landed on
his back; the snarling mother, her teeth bared and
claws tearing the shirt off his back. Then it made off
leaving Dick with his first captive marten. He has
discovered much about the animals since then, and
tipped me off where best I might see them.

The spot he recommended was a roadside litter-bin

overleaf: The country of Torridon and Loch Maree

at dusk. And two nights in succession I saw the chocolate coloured animal which is bigger than a ferret, with a pale bib and pointed ears. As it darted across the road and sprang onto the bin my impression was of a lithe cat moving on air, like a flickering shadow rather than something substantial.

The clue to its speed is the muscular legs and protruding claws on the large pads. Faster than a squirrel in the trees, or a roe deer on the ground, it can outclimb or outrun both. And it ranges right to the hilltops, searching after small birds or voles. But at the litter bins Dick Balharry has seen them eating orange peel, cake, jam or anything else that was going. They will also box moths out of the air, eat any kind of wild berry, and catch sea-trout by waiting and pouncing like bears. Balharry has even seen one swim a loch, and at the time of writing they appear regularly at a window of Loch Maree hotel for scraps.

The country all round Loch Maree is a reservoir of Highland wild-life. Black-throated and red-throated divers, greenshank, peregrine falcons, golden eagles, dunlin and golden plover are among the breeding birds. Otter, wild cat, roe and red deer, badger and fox range the loch shores. Alas, the ospreys which used

The crofts lie on the sea fringes of Loch Ewe

to nest on Eilean Suthainn, and on a promontory opposite Isle Maree have not yet returned since the days when Osgood Mackenzie robbed their nests.

But there are indications that the birds may yet recolonise territories which have been vacant since the turn of the century. After all, Mackenzie thought he had exterminated the pine marten after taking 40–50 skins every year to make sables and coats. The animal was down to a danger point with only one known stronghold in treeless Sutherland. Now it is on the increase in many places, thanks to forestry and a more tolerant attitude towards it. The osprey too is coming back, and spreading out from Speyside.

Mackenzie, the author of *A hundred years in the Highlands* and creator of Inverewe Gardens, had the winter shooting of the islands of Loch Maree in 1858, and so vivid is his writing of his days with dog and gun that I sometimes fancy I have seen him and his black setter Fan edging stealthily through the pines of the twenty-five islands, the dog pointing at a blackcock nibbling catkins off a treetop while Osgood, gun on shoulder, knocks it into the air.

It was the potato famine of 1846–8 which caused the road to be built along the west shore of Loch Maree. Osgood Mackenzie writes: 'But for the potato blight, when should we have got our roads made through the

The house Osgood Mackenzie built on rocks, where he created a famous garden

country? My mother never left Gairloch, not even for a day, for three long years when the famine was at its height.'

That resourceful lady put all the able-bodied men on her land to work, paying them a wage which enabled them to live. Little Osgood was allowed to cut the first turf, surrounded by starving Skyemen. In those bad times it was necessary to dole out oatmeal to keep the coastal crofters from starving, when their only standby was shellfish boiled in milk. Osgood's mother rode her horse everywhere at this time of desperation, acting as doctor, building nine or ten schools in which the Gaelic language had to come first, and influencing people to pull down their insanitary dwellings and build new ones with timbers which she provided.

Under the run-rig system houses were huddled together because the crofting land was communally held. She reorganised it by giving each crofter a four

The rock basin of the Gorm Loch near Lochan Fada, with Slioch (left)
Ben Lair (centre)

acre piece. I think that good lady would be impressed if she were able to visit the houses now, all rebuilt, and with electric light, bathrooms, comfortable furniture, carpets, television sets and telephones.

Osgood himself forecast that more education would mean less cultivation and in his lifetime saw the crofts go back as people became less willing to spend all their time with crowbar and handplough. The croft lands lie mainly on the coastal fringes of Loch Ewe, and nowadays they do little more than feed a cow and provide some vegetables and potatoes. Like most people the crofters depend upon wage packets nowadays, and the boarding of summer visitors provides a good supplement to their income.

Loch Tollaidh

Not a notable loch, but an interesting one historically, for it was events sparked off on the artificial island, or crannog, which divested the Gairloch lands from the

Macleods and passed them to the Mackenzies. This is the loch you pass on the drive over the moor between Gairloch and Poolewe, and it is worth pausing to look at the rocky setting and the peaks of the A'Mhaighdean wilderness which stretches behind. And if the time be sunset and crimson from the west is flooding into the loch, it is symbolic of the murders between rival factions in the clan feuding days.

The events here happened in the early fifteenth century when the Macleods of Lewis, brothers to the chief, sailed east to Gairloch to kill three sons of a marriage between a Macleod of Gairloch and a Mackenzie of Kintail—both of noble blood. The Macleod had remarried, and had a daughter by his second wife. Fearing his enemies he took refuge with the family on the crannog on Loch Tollie. Unfortunately for him, he went fishing in the River Ewe, and was taking a nap when he was surprised by the Lewis Macleods who chopped off his head.

Then they made their way to the island to tear the tainted children away from the widow. Luckily, only two of the boys were present. They were seized and stabbed to death in a glen near Poolewe. But the mother got the blood-stained shirts as evidence to take to Edinburgh. A commission of fire and sword was granted to the Mackenzies against the Macleods, and also the lands of Gairloch. The two murderers were caught and killed, but it was a long time before all the Macleods were driven out.

The saga of retribution would take a long time to tell, but it was well remembered, and Osgood Mackenzie, son of the twelfth chief of Gairloch wrote in 1921:

'I have occasion very frequently to pass the little island in Loch Tollie . . . And though I have been passing there now for over 70 years, I never do so without realising that but for the tragedy of the island in Loch Tollie, we should never have been Mackenzies of Gairloch, my nephew would not be Sir Kenneth Mackenzie, seventh baronet of Gairloch and thirteenth in direct succession to Hector Roy, and I should not be at Inverewe.'

Loch Tollaidh is a rock basin in sheared and folded Lewisian gneiss. Elliptical in shape it is just under a mile long, with a maximum breadth of 800 yds and a maximum depth in the centre of 86 ft. Once there was a dam at the outlet stream, to maintain the water at a higher level and release enough to power a mill-wheel as required.

If the day is fine you will be rewarded if you leave your car eastward of the loch, and take a walk down the farm track to Tollie Bay, or climb the nearest hillock for a view of Loch Maree, the wild and beautiful hinterland which afforded the energetic Mackenzie such delight to the end of his days, though his living memorial is Inverewe Gardens which he created out of little more than rock and peat.

It was the creation of something out of nothing which was the basis of Mackenzie's philosophy. He loved craftsmanship, the skills of the hands, whether applied to building, agriculture, fishing or shooting, especially when it was a game of wits. And he was a patient man, waiting 20 years for the trees he planted to grow up, so that he could build a garden in their shelter, a garden that is a wonder of the world, growing sub-tropical and other plants on a barren peninsula of Torridonian sandstone swept by Atlantic winds.

It was when Mackenzie was excavating the foundations for his house on Am Ploc–The High Hump–he found that the ground was unexpectedly soft below. It was a former seabeach, three parts pebbles, one part blackish earth, so he wheeled out thousands of barrow loads of stones, picking them like potatoes, dumped them in the sea, replacing them with cartloads of soil carried from long distances. Even the blue clay marl from the seashore, full of decayed oyster shells and crabs, was spread on his prepared ground.

He tells the story of how when cutting a 12-ft-deep bank above the garden to make a terrace he came across the deep holes of a former badger set, and from it came raspberry seedlings where none had grown before. He presumes the badgers had eaten the fruit and the seeds had been waiting centuries to germinate. It was a foretaste of what his remarkable garden was to produce once he had provided the sheltering trees.

He was eventually able to boast that anything that will grow in Britain will thrive here, yet all that was growing when he started were two dwarf willows. The Eucalyptus trees he planted are over 90 ft high now and the whole garden is the subject of a fine book, *Inverewe* by May Cowan.

See it in the rather colourless Highland spring if you would fully appreciate the miracle that Mackenzie wrought with sheltering shrubs and woods to provide micro climates for early flowers from all over the world, dwarf daffodils from the Atlas Mountains, lustrous yellow beneath multi-coloured rhododendrons from the Himalayas, and above them both the great magnolia in flower overhead – all this on what used to be windswept headland – vivid with colour in contrast to the snow on the great wall of the Torridon peaks.

Mackenzie created it, but he also destroyed a great deal at the same time. Listen to his words as he gives the figures from his game book for one year, 1868. Grouse, 1313; black game, 33; patridges, 49; golden plover, 110; wild duck, 35; snipe, 53; rock pigeons, 91; hares, 184; a total of 1900 head without mentioning geese, teal, ptarmigan and roe. He writes: 'What a big pile it would make if all the black game I shot between 1855 and 1900 were gathered in one heap. Now alas! there are none, and why, who can tell?'

Mackenzie did not appreciate that it was precisely because game was so plentiful that there was so much of what he called 'vermin' on his ground. Like all the shooting men of his time he thought that by poisoning and trapping golden eagles, foxes, badgers, otters, wildcats, pine martens and polecats he would see a big increase in birds. Even killing 34 golden eagles in four seasons had little effect however. All his long life he waged war on 'vermin' yet his game continued to decline. What had gone wrong was the total environment, due to the destruction of the woods and overgrazing by sheep. The rich capital of game had been expended.

Yet Mackenzie was himself a conservationist, for he deplored the misuse of land going on around him. Undoubtedly he loved wildlife, even when the smoke was puffing out of his gun as he dropped a whooper swan or a snipe. The general decline he saw around him was due to massive deforestation, soil impoverishment due to muirburn. He would be enthusiastic about the efforts of the Nature Conservancy if he were alive today, I am sure. And he would be forced to admit the truth that it is the prey which controls the predator, and not the other way round.

Yet one can never be sure, for there are still some landowners in the Highlands who wage war on noble predators, when they should regard them as indicators that there is game for the killing on the ground. After

all it is in countries where game is most plentiful
that there is the greatest numbers of birds of prey – as
in Turkey and East Africa for example.

Lochan Fada

North-east of Loch Maree lies an interesting long
loch with a contradictory name, Lochan Fada,
contradictory because the word Lochan usually
refers to a small loch, more in the nature of a tarn,
whereas Fada means long. There are many Loch
Fadas in Scotland, but this one happens to be the
biggest of its name in the country. Length $3\frac{3}{4}$ miles,
maximum breadth $\frac{2}{3}$ mile, with a maximum depth of
248 ft, it could hardly be called small. It is a rock
basin lying between 3,000-ft hills, deeper at the lower
end where the glacier ice excavated a fault.

Seen from the top of Slioch you appreciate its
setting in the jumble of peaks which thrust between
here and Loch Broom, where only footpaths thread
the wilderness. No other piece of undeveloped
country like it remains in Scotland, and it is my hope
that nothing will change it. No one lives permanently
within it. It is deer forest and fishing country *par
excellence*. The crags offer some of the finest climbing
in Scotland. The walking routes are without compare.

The easiest way to see Lochan Fada is to walk from
Kinlochewe on the old drove road to Loch Maree, as
if you were going to climb Slioch, and branch right
up Glen Bianasdail after crossing the stream. You
can see the ruins of the iron works building here,
and the shore below is known to this day as Cladh
nan Sussanach – the Englishman's graveyard. The
glen you follow up is narrow and walled by steep
crags on the right; it is a hanging valley where a
corrie glacier continued to dig deep after Loch
Maree had been formed. The stream drains out of
Lochan Fada so all you have to do is follow up the
good path.

The whole atmosphere is impressive, looking out
from the defile, back to the grey peaks of Beinn Eighe
and its Caledonian pines fronting Loch Maree. Then
after climbing to 1,250 feet you drop to the rather
bleak head of the lochan. The best of it lies west, and
if you are a strong walker you should go along 3 miles
and come back by a fine path which climbs to 1,750 ft,
dropping by Loch Garbhaig and the Furnace
Burn. True you have more than this distance to walk

back along Loch Maree to regain your route of the morning, but the path winding through the natural oaks contouring up and down should not be missed.

Lochan Fada occupies a pre-Torridonian valley which has been re-exposed by the removal of great masses of sandstone by glacier action. The mixture revealed now is Lewisian gneiss with on top of the bed-rock the remaining Torridonian sandstone. The narrow shape of the loch means that only a limited surface is exposed to heating agencies. This allied to its height above sea-level means it is colder at all depths than Loch Maree.

An attentive look east reveals that the natural drainage line from Lochan Fada was once eastwards, until down-cutting by the stream in Glen Bianasdail excavated a new outlet and lowered the level of the entire loch, leaving the old drainage line in Gleann na Muice without a head. The evidence can be read in the streams, especially if you return to your base via the Heights of Kinlochewe. The two little lochans immediately east of the Lochan Fada and at a slightly higher elevation were submerged in Lochan Fada, most probably, before the level was lowered. A track from here leads south-eastwards to the Heights of Kinlochewe. The total round by the routes described is about 14 miles.

A longer and better expedition however is to follow the south shore of Lochan Fada westwards where it ends below the spectacular cliffs of Ben Lair in narrow Gleann Tulacha – a wild and splendid place quite the opposite to the bleak eastern end. The most rewarding thing to do here is cross the stream north and climb a thousand feet to the ridge of Beinn Tarsuinn Chaol to look into the splendid rock basin of the Gorm Loch Mor beneath A'Mhaighdean.

The ridge is knife-edged, but without difficulty, though the slopes falling to the Gorm Loch are rocky. The savagery of the scene is heightened by the extreme loneliness of the country, no easy way out in any direction. The north face of Slioch rises in great ribs of pink sandstone, but all else around is gneiss, though the north-easterly peaks are capped with Cambrian quartzite. Even the head of Loch Coruisk in Skye has not more character.

After seeing the west end of Lochan Fada there is an exciting way back, by swinging away south-westwards just over one mile from the end of the loch on a good track which climbs to 1,800 ft. It leads you back to Loch Maree via Loch Garbhaig, whose outlet is the Furnace Burn dropping 1,000 ft to the oakwoods of the shore. The remains of the old iron-works are still visible.

Loch Garbhaig has a fishing bothy on the west shore and a large island half a mile from it. It is a bare loch, though evidence of tree stumps in the bogs show there must have been a fair amount of woodland on the southern approaches. The loch is just over 1 mile long with a maximum breadth of $\frac{1}{4}$ mile and a maximum depth of 93 ft. Despite being the same level as Lochan Fada it was found to be 4 degrees warmer.

In 1963 there was a North of Scotland Hydro-Electric Board Construction Scheme drawn up to connect Lochan Fada and Loch Garbhaig by tunnel and operate them as a reservoir, the water to be taken to an underground power station near Furnace. This Scheme, which would also have harnessed the Fionn Loch as a reservoir, never came to pass for reasons of cost weighed against alternative means of generation. It was a carefully thought-out scheme designed with high regard to amenity in a uniquely wild and beautiful wilderness, almost the last of its kind in Britain.

Miraculously, it was reprieved, and there is a growing body of opinion who believe that such a pristine piece of roadless wilderness should be preserved against development for all time, accessible only to those who are prepared to make the effort of getting there on foot. The country we have discussed is only a small part of it. The northern part of it, from the Fionn Loch to Little Loch Broom, comes under the lochs of the Gruinard Basin.

Loch Clair and Loch Coulin

In the juxtaposition of Liathach with Loch Clair nature has excelled herself in providing a perfect mirror for a rock peak of impressive bulk rising '. . . from river bed to the sky, Grey courses of masonry tier on tier, And pinnacle riven on high'. Set amongst birches and Caledonian pines in Glen Torridon, said to be the oldest glen in the world, Loch Clair has great atmosphere. Loch Coulin is simply an appendage of it, on the walkers' track that runs over the Coulin Pass to Achnashellach. The drainage of the lochs is by the Allt Ghairbhe into

Loch Clair and the Peak of Liathach

Loch Maree, and there is a direct footpath from
Loch Coulin north to Kinlochewe.

This too is Mackenzie country, and of all their lands
from Kintail to Loch Broom this is the most spectacular, and the most poverty stricken, for it has been well
said that the noblest scenery makes the poorest agriculture. The exposure of rock to grass shows what a
hard country this is, but compared with the rest of
Glen Torridon, Lochs Clair and Coulin are sylvan,
hence their impact–especially in winter when the
summit ridges are snow capped and the rocks are
bare, rising a full 3,000 ft above the low glen.

The skyline of peaks lying north across Glen
Torridon is the nearest thing we have in Scotland to a
National Park, with the Nature Conservancy owning
the easterly section and the National Trust for Scot-
land the westerly peaks including the summits of
Liathach, Beinn Alligin, parts of Beinn Dearg and

The hidden north face of Liathach easily reached by path

Beinn Eighe. With camping grounds, information centres and nature trails it means the minimum of restrictions in a wild country which used to be sacred to deer stalking.

Lochs Clair and Coulin are on private land and there is no right of way for cars on the narrow track to the Lodge. It is no hardship to walk in a place where there is so much to see of geological and naturalist interest, for this is classic country for Highland birds and mammals, where greenshank and black-throated divers nest, otters have their holts and pine martens their dens.

Loch Clair is only separated from Loch Coulin by an alluvial fan which has been built up by the stream coming in on the west, the Allt na Luib, otherwise they are one loch damned by morainic drift, even the two small islands on Loch Clair are moraines. The depth of 93 ft maximum for Loch Clair occurs in the deeper

Summit ridge Liathach

water of the south-eastern portion, the total length
being 1⅓ miles, with a maximum breadth of 300 yds.
The mean depth is 42 ft.

Loch Coulin lies 300 yds over alluvial ground and it
too is 1⅓ miles long, with a maximum breadth of ⅓ of a
mile, but with a maximum depth of only 49 ft. It is
irregular in bottom compared to Clair, being cut into
three basins, the deepest being in the broad south-
eastern portion. The north-westerly basin is 32 ft in
maximum depth, and the central basin 22 ft.

Going west down Glen Torridon a pause should be
made opposite the small Lochan an Iasgaich to look
at the sea of hummocky moraines above the climbers'
cottage. It is called Coire a' Cheud-chnoic,—'Corrie
of the Hundred Hills', and it is well named. You could
do worse than leave your car here, and walk north up
the path signposted Coire Dhu to see the hidden face
of Liathach which is even sheerer and more fretted

Ben Eighe Deer Park, Loch Maree

than its other side.

Better still you could leave this path at the lochans and slant in to Loch Coire Mhic Fhearchair over rough ground where the dwarf cornel grows. The stream pouring out of the gap between Sail Mor and Ruadh Stac Mor leads you to the dark loch and the most remarkable piece of rock architecture in Scotland, three pillars of pale quartzite standing on a base of wine-red Torridonian sandstone, the line of separation at near mid-height as definite and contrasting as icing on a cake. Except that this cake is over 1,000 ft sheer and looks out over a waste of lochs and moors stretching seawards or to Loch Maree.

I do not know any other place in Scotland to equal this for wild austerity, or for adventure if you are a climbing man. I have had the pleasure of making new routes here, but much exploration still remains to be done on the great triple buttresses.

Loch Kernsary

Osgood Mackenzie tells the story of his early sporting days and ends with a tale of the only good shot he ever had at swans.

'There were three whoopers out in the middle of the loch, [Loch Kernsary] when a very violent squall came on, with sleet and hail. We noticed the swans come in for shelter under a promontory that jutted out into the loch, so we ran to circumvent them, and I killed one on the water and wounded another as it rose. The latter we had to chase in a boat, and whilst we were doing so the third one passed high over the boat, and I brought it down.'

It would not only be unsporting, but against the law to kill whooper swans now, and I thought of Osgood when I was at Kernsary on a wild March day and came on three whooper swans, the only sign of life in a desolate country on the moor above Poolewe. You can drive to Kernsary, on payment of a 50p fee to use the rough road, or walk the footpath which leads to the west end in a mile and a half from Poolewe.

The loch drains into the bottom of Loch Maree opposite Tollie Bay, and is the most southerly of a whole scatter of good but bleak fishing lochs. This loch of many inlets is distinguished by having a crannog–an artificial island–near its south-western shore, but unlike the one in Loch Tollie it has no history. A track runs along its north side into the great wilderness behind Slioch, a place purring with dunlin and piping golden plover in summer.

Low lying, Loch Kernsary is roughly $1\frac{2}{3}$ miles long and $\frac{1}{2}$ a mile in maximum breadth, with a greatest depth of 93 ft in the north-west, 250 yds from the shore. Apart from its irregular shape it has four basins each deeper than 50 ft on a floor of mixed Lewisian gneiss and Torridonian sandstone. The ice markings on the rocks known as 'Striae' lie parallel to these 50-ft basins.

Loch Ghiuragarstidh drains into Loch Kernsary and lies half a mile to the north. Small as it is, only 1,200 yds long and 370 yds at its broadest, it has little islands with pine trees, and boulders and reefs in its southern half give a clue to its shallowness. In fact all but 4 per cent is covered by less than 25 ft of water. The maximum depth is 37 ft, in the northern part.

Loch a' Bhaid Luachriach. There is a path to this

loch from Aultbea where it is known locally as the Goose Loch, and the local hotel has the brown trout fishing rights. Shaped like the wings of a butterfly, it is almost two lochs, with a little connected body-piece. The length is over $1\frac{1}{2}$ miles with a maximum breadth of over 1 mile. The north-east is a simple basin reaching a depth of 143 ft in its centre. The south-west is an irregular basin, with a maximum depth of 43 ft. The connection between the two is only 15 ft wide.

Loch Mhic Ille Riabhaich lies a mile or so south-east of the last named loch on a path climbing over a shoulder of low hill. Its main interest, apart from fishing, is the remains of a strong point on one of its little islands, nothing about which is known. Half a mile in length and just a bit less in breadth it is mostly shallow, the maximum depth being only 12 ft.

Loch nan Dailthean on the Poolewe–Aultbea road is even shallower though it is $\frac{1}{2}$ a mile long.

The northerly arms which enclose Loch Ewe have other shallow lochs. The easterly arm has Loch an t'Slagain near Slaggan Bay which receives the outflow of several smaller lochs to the east and south. Its length is $\frac{2}{3}$ of a mile by $\frac{1}{3}$ of a mile, with a maximum depth of 55 ft to the south-east. Aultbea Hotel has the fishing rights, and the best brown trout season is from June until August.

Loch Sguod is on the other side of Loch Ewe, on the western arm and is shallow, reaching a maximum depth of no more than 14 ft. The length is $\frac{3}{4}$ of a mile and the breadth $\frac{1}{2}$ a mile. Right out north-west of it extending to the point are other lochs, the biggest of which is Loch an Drainc, length $\frac{3}{4}$ of a mile by $\frac{1}{3}$ of a mile in maximum breadth and with a maximum depth of 55 ft. Mixed woodlands, steep little knolls and moorland gives great character to this interesting area right out on the tip of Loch Ewe.

The Dubh Loch (left) and the Fionn Loch from A' Mhaighdean

Ben Airidh Charr (centre) where white-tailed eagle nested, Fionn Loch

Lochs of the Gruinard Basin

Fionn Loch, Dubh Loch, Lochs Beannach, na Moine Buige, Eileach Mhic 'ille Riabhaich, Fada, na Beiste, na Sealga (Sheallag)

Fionn Loch means the White Loch and Osgood Mackenzie devotes a chapter of *A Hundred Years in the Highlands* to it. He calls it '. . . the best trout loch in Scotland', and supports the assertion with evidence of catches. He writes of a weighing-in. 'There were four beauties lying side by side on the table of the small drinking-room, and they turned the scale at 51 pounds. The total weight of the twelve fish caught that 12th April day by trolling was 87 pounds 12 ounces.' Osgood didn't catch them, but he missed 'The biggest fish I ever saw on that loch . . . I was casting with a light rod, and had on an ordinary cast with three small flies, just where the small burn flows into the loch at the Feith a Chaisgan sandy bay, when I hooked an enormous fish . . . double the size of any we had seen before. It jumped three times clean out of the water close to the boat, and we saw it as well as if we had handled it; but in spite of us all doing our very best to ease the tension on the line, it soon carried off everything. Without in the least wishing to exaggerate, I honestly declare that fish to have been a twenty-five pounder.'

Big fish are still plentiful in the Fionn Loch, and permission should be sought at Kernsary, a keeper's cottage approached by a private road out of Poolewe. A payment is demanded at Kernsary if you wish to leave a car. The track continues north-eastwards over the moor for another 3 miles to the strange world of the Fionn Loch.

The lookout here from the boathouse is strangely reminiscent of Rannoch Moor, with heathery islands and rocks and headlands giving the impression of a watery maze. But this loch is infinitely more dramatic than anything on Rannoch, for although its north-western end is among low hills, it ends eastward in great cliffs and bluffs of the wildest gneiss mountains in Scotland. The rampart forms a horse-shoe, which is the heart of the Fada-Fionn wilderness mentioned in the last chapter.

You can walk from Kernsary on a footpath all the way to the head of the loch, but a much better way of letting the Fionn Loch make its impact is to walk from

Letterewe on the east shore of Loch Maree, and cross the high Bealach Mheinnidh on the bridle path and suddenly come upon what is perhaps the most striking change of scene in Scotland, with the Fionn Loch laid out like a map before you, while on all sides of you there are wild cliffs. The path leads down to a little causeway separating Dubh Loch from the Fionn Loch. And over the other side lies the lonely white house of Carn More, no longer permanently occupied, but used as a shooting box in the stalking season.

I remember the MacRae family who used to stay here telling me how they had boated their possessions up the $5\frac{3}{4}$ miles of loch to its head, almost foundering on the way when a squall struck them. Calum, the father, was deer stalker to the Marquis of Zetland in those days, and Andy, the possessor of a school leaving certificate, was paid a small sum to teach his two young sisters, Katy and Mary. Young Calum acted as ghillie and handyman to his father. And genial Mrs MacRae generated more good nature about her than any person I have met before or since. It was a house of laughter where I stayed as a guest, helped to build paths, and rode the Highland pony called Dick.

Dick carried the provisions across the Bealach or helped bring home the peats. The little stone bothy below the house is the same that Osgood Mackenzie slept in, wrapped in his blankets as a boy of 16, an occasion which he described as among the happiest, if not the very happiest day of his life. Lying on the floor beside a fire of bog fir he was full of excitement because he had bought for £5 the right to stalk deer over the 50,000 acres of the Strath na Sheallag – 'The Valley of Hunting'. It was Mackenzie who built the private road to the loch from Kernsary.

In his day the white-tailed eagle nested on a small island until the constant robbing of the nest forced them on to the cliff of Beinn Airidh Charr, not inaccessible enough, unfortunately, for the shepherd took the two big white eggs and sold them to little Osgood. Suffolk egg collectors robbed the ospreys which nested hereabouts, and nowadays the only island breeders of particular interest are the black-throated divers and the herons.

The maximum width of the $5\frac{3}{8}$-mile-long Fionn Loch is $1\frac{1}{2}$ miles, and the maximum depth of 144 ft occurs in two places, near the south-eastern end, and in the central part opposite Lochan Beannach. The

The Fuar Loch beneath the rocks of A' Mhaighdean

bottom is extremely irregular, and although boulders protrude, there may be deep water each side of them. The northerly fish tail reaches a depth of 97 ft, while its more westerly prolongation is 78 ft maximum.

Under the North of Scotland Hydro-Electric Board scheme it was proposed to build a 25-ft dam below the outlet of the Fionn Loch, together with a cut-off dam to the north, and thus raise the loch 11 ft, tapping it by tunnel to an underground power station at Furnace on Loch Maree. The gain in electricity would not have balanced the loss in wilderness character which is unique in Scotland.

The voice of this place in summer is the triple staccato of the greenshank, the piping of golden plover, the 'reeling' of dunlin, the singing of meadow pipits and the twittering of twites. Golden eagle, peregrine falcon and raven live on the crags. It is to

overleaf: Loch na Sealga (Sheallag) fed by remote streams

be hoped that the motor car will never invade this sanctuary.

Dubh Loch. Only the width of a man-made causeway separates the Fionn Loch and the Dubh Loch, and in very high water they may become one. Litigation in the court decided that these lochs were one, but the House of Lords overturned the decision, so Dubh Loch has the status of separate loch. Certainly the mile-and-a-quarter dark loch has a character of its own, penetrating as it does into the rocks which rise steeply from its shore in places. Even the shape of the loch, at an angle to the Fionn Loch, gives it the feel of a corrie lochan in such stark surroundings. High above it, from the house of Carn More, contours the climbing path to the Strath na Sheallag. Ideally you should walk over it to Dundonnel on Little Loch Broom if you get this far.

The Dubh Loch is only $\frac{2}{5}$ of a mile in maximum breadth with a greatest depth of 88 ft in the centre. In contrast to the irregular Fionn Loch the Dubh Loch is a simple basin, though there is a bank of shallow water about 300 yds from the south-eastern end. At one point in this shoaling there is only 2 ft of water though it drops to 20 ft each side of it. There is a stalkers' path along the south side of the Dubh Loch leading into a wild recess below A'Mhaighdean. Follow this up and you are at the Gorm Loch Mor only a short distance from Lochan Fada.

A strong walker could explore all of this from Kinlochewe, though the ideal is to carry food and a sleeping bag and have a night in the bothy at Carn More. But you have to be entirely self-supporting.

Loch Beannach, Loch na Moine Buige, Loch Eileach Mhic 'ille Riabhaich, Loch Fada and Loch na Beiste are other lochs of the Gruinard Basin, the first four peppering the region of the Fionn Loch among many others. The last named lies north of Laide on the western arm of Gruinard Bay. Details are as follows.

Loch Beannach lies close to the western shore of the Fionn Loch at a point about half way along its length. It is an irregular and complicated loch with sinuosities which almost cut it in two. Measurement is difficult because of the shape but the surveyors gave the maximum depth as 27 feet. Islands and rocks show that it is very shallow, and in fact the mean depth is only $6\frac{1}{2}$ ft.

Loch na Moine Buige is almost part of the Fionn Loch westerly extremity, and has a depth of 60 ft maximum and a mean of $24\frac{1}{2}$ ft. Length $\frac{3}{4}$ of a mile, it is $\frac{1}{4}$ of a mile broad, so can be considered deep for its dimensions.

Loch Eileach Mhic 'ille Riabhaich. This is where the Fionn Loch spills out and makes a small loch before becoming a river by dropping over two water-falls. Length is $\frac{3}{4}$ of a mile and it is less than $\frac{1}{4}$ of a mile broad, with a maximum depth of 33 ft in its widest part.

Loch Fada. Yet another loch of this name and a longish loch lying north-north-west of the Fionn Loch. Length $1\frac{1}{2}$ miles, it has a few good islands on it. Half a mile in maximum breadth it is 56 ft deep near the wide central portion, though the mean is only 17 ft.

Loch na Beiste. Situated on the Rubha Mor where there are many little lochs of its kind. This one gets the name from a beast which was thought to live there, but when the owner tried to drain the loch to reveal its secret he failed. The moon casting its shadow on two stones, giving it the shape of an animal, is thought to be the true explanation of the beast. It is a simple loch 35 ft at its deepest, and a $\frac{1}{3}$ of a mile long by $\frac{1}{4}$ of a mile broad.

Loch na Sealga. (SHEALLAG) This superb loch spills into the Gruinard River but is fed by the streams from some of the remotest hills in Scotland. Domin-ated by the pinnacles of An Teallach on the north, and Ben Dearg Mor and Beag to the south, the problem of the traveller making his way against the grain of the country is to ford the broad feeder river, the Abhainn Strath na Sealga.

It should be waded where it is broadest, north-west of the join with Gleann na Muice Beag, and if the time of year is outwith the deer stalking season, you can be sure of a roof over your head at Shenavall. It is no more than a bothy, so you need sleeping bag and food. A good track from here leads across the shoulder of An Teallach to the Dundonnel road.

The loch contains good fish, salmon, sea trout, brown trout and char but is preserved. The deepest part of the $3\frac{1}{8}$-mile loch is a mile from the inflow where it goes down to 217 ft and is flat bottomed over the wide south-eastern portion, getting shallower as the loch narrows, reaching less than 50 ft in its last mile.

Strath na Sealga, or Sheallag, 'The Valley of Hunting', is on the line of the cattle droving road from Gruinard Bay, swinging south by the Lochan an Nid to Loch a' Bhraoin and the Dirrie Mor to Garve.

At the head of the loch, and east to the empty house of Achneigie and beyond, it is a green pleasant place with scattered birches, in contrast to the Torridonian slopes above with their pink terraces of sandstone and striking moraines. The wild glens leading in every direction give it an air of mystery, since none have roads leading through them. The bare slabs breaking through the soil, with their litter of erratic blocks like curling stones add the final primeval touches.

One last word. If you should make your way out of this wilderness northward on the fine track to Little Loch Broom, make a divergence to Loch Toll an Lochan if the weather is right, for here is the only rival to Loch Coire Mhic Fearchair of Beinn Eighe. The difference here is that the rock is all sandstone, rising in fierce pinnacles and towers 1,500 ft over the tiny oval of the lochan. Go there in late autumn when the stags are roaring and the wild bellowing is the right accompaniment to such a place. The walking is remarkably easy, and the descent on the track swift.

Lochs of the Conon Basin

Lochs Droma, Glascarnoch, Vaich, Luichart, Orrin, Fannich, Gowan, Beannachan, Garve, Achilty, Glass and Morie

Loch Droma on the Dirrie Mor on the heights between Ullapool and Garve belonged to the Loch Broom drainage until captured by the North of Scotland Hydro-Electric Board as part of their Conon Valley Scheme which harnesses the catchment of the Fannich Mountains and the lochs of Strath Bran, together with some completely new lochs like Glascarnoch and Vaich to the north of Garve by Altguish Inn.

Loch Droma occupies the glacial breach where the ice broke through to Loch Broom, but had been enlarged artificially even before Hydro-Electric Board alterations. It was less dreary in the old days when it had a good stand of firs on its north side. In those days the length was $1\frac{1}{4}$ miles by $\frac{1}{4}$ mile maximum breadth with the greatest depth 16 ft. It is smaller today, at a mile long by $\frac{1}{5}$ of a mile broad, the new area being 103 acres compared to the old of 116 acres. With a spillway level of 883 ft O.D., the maximum depth can hardly have changed.

Bleak as it is, with high peaks on each side, Loch Droma points west to An Teallach, and when this peak is mirrored in the loch at sunset the effect is of remarkable beauty. It is no longer the 'Destitution Road'. That name which still sticks was not given because of the scenic bleakness, but because it was the road taken by the destitute crofters driven out by hard times and political pressure.

The water from Droma, formerly outflowing to the north-west, now feeds eastward into what used to be, the Glascarnoch River valley but is now occupied by a large reservoir called Loch Glascarnoch impounded by a big concrete dam above Altguish Inn. The spillway level here is 826 ft, and the length of the loch is nearly $4\frac{1}{2}$ miles by 1 mile greatest breadth, though the mean breadth is just over $\frac{1}{2}$ a mile. The capacity of the reservoir is 17,132,000,000 gallons.

Going north from Garve to Ullapool you motor along the south shore of this reservoir which is fed by tunnel from another new reservoir to the north called Loch Vaich, whose spillway is 840 ft and the highest storage reservoir in the Conon scheme. Loch Vaich is

Loch Glascarnoch, a hydro-electric reservoir on the Garve – Ullapool road

Loch Luichart and pipes to the power station

just under $3\frac{1}{2}$ miles long and just over $\frac{1}{3}$ of a mile in maximum breadth with a capacity of 2,470,000,000 gallons.

The water from Loch Vaich goes through a small power station at the outlet of the tunnel which carries it to Glascarnoch, the power generated being carried by submarine cable across Glascarnoch to be delivered into the distribution system. Between these high lochs and the tail race of the Torr Achilty power station there is a drop of 830 ft, and all but a few feet is harnessed as the waters pass through three sets of turbines at different levels, Mossford, Luichart and Torr Achilty.

The total scheme is a complicated one harnessing 345 sq. miles of catchment to produce about 290 million units of electricity yearly. There are seven generating stations, seven main dams, 20 miles of tunnels and 15 miles of aqueducts, not to mention 30 miles of public and private roads and a main line railway station.

Loch Glascarnoch is impounded behind 1,670 ft of dam, 92 ft high, and the tunnel which carries its waters to Mossford power station on Loch Luichart is nearly 5 miles in a drop of 530 ft. The site of this power station has grim associations with the force of water, for the original clachan which stood here was obliterated by floods, it is said. The water which falls today produces about 112 million units of electricity.

When Loch Luichart was a natural loch its measurements were 5 miles by 1 mile in maximum breadth, with a maximum depth of 164 ft and a mean of 67 ft. The 45-foot-high dam built at its outlet and stretching 680 ft raised it by 40 ft to 6 miles though the breadth remains approximately 1 mile. The capacity is estimated at 37,160,000,000 gallons.

The attractive feature of Loch Luichart is its almost Perthshire character, with heather and fine mixed woods to give its low hills colour. Its Highland impact is all the greater because it contrasts so much with the big fields and agricultural lands of the Moray Firth. And as you climb away westward the vegetation changes, brilliantly in autumn when the birches are golden and heather and bracken are rusting.

From the dam the water passes to the Luichart Power Station at the junction of the Meig with the Conon, a fine building in Tarradale stone generating 124 million units of electricity. The big pipelines

Low water at Loch Fannich Rockfill dam

supplying the station are invisible, buried in the hillside behind the station. Good taste here, like the Meig
dam nearby, tunnelling water to top-up Loch Luichart
from a narrow reservoir.

The Torr Achilty power house is similar to the one
at Pitlochry, in that the dam and power house are in
one unit. It not only uses water discharged from all
the lochs mentioned, but gets an additional supply
from the Orrin power station to the west, to boost the
output by 5 million units of electricity.

The Orrin generating station in Strath Conon gets
its water supply from a new loch formed behind a dam
five miles upstream from the Orrin Falls. This new
loch is 5½ miles long by over ½ a mile broad and has a
capacity of 13,020,000,000 gallons. The Orrin reservoir is in bare hills, with a spillway level of 840 ft. The
dam is 130 ft high on one side of a hill and 50 ft high
on the other, the two sections totalling over 2,000 ft.
Over 4 miles of tunnel takes the water to the power

Loch a' Chroisg between Achnasheen and Kinlochewe

house on Loch Acholockie, the small loch formed by the Torr Achilty dam.

Grasping all this is none too easy, but it is not the whole story. We have still to deal with Loch Fannich remotely situated beneath high mountains and the largest loch within the Cromarty Firth drainage basin. This is in the heart of deer forest country, and has a lodge on its shores which can be reached by private road from Grudie, just west of Loch Luichart. It is a lonely wild track climbing up to over 800 ft with steep rocky peaks rising on the north side.

Good for trout fishing, the old length of the loch was 7 miles by $\frac{3}{4}$ of a mile, with a maximum depth of 282 ft and a mean depth of 109 ft. The rockfill dam built to increase its capacity has increased the length by only half a mile, and the breadth by almost nothing. The surface area today is 2,710 acres compared to the natural 2,300 acres in pre-hydro-electric days. It is a true rock basin of simple form with lots of morainic

47

debris above it on the hills.

The tunnel which leads four miles through the hills to the power station at Grudie Bridge became notable for 'Operation Bathplug'. This was the final blowing out of the 600-ton plug of rock 81 ft below the surface of Loch Fannich through which the water would gush. The underground explosion successfully pulled the plug, and the storage capacity of Loch Fannich today is worth 102 million units of electricity. The neat power station of pink tinged stone is at the west end of Loch Luichart.

Just south of it is the Achanalt Power Station using a barrage with sluice gates across the outlet of Loch a' Chuilinn to regulate the River Bran. The effect has been to combine shallow Loch Achanalt with deeper Loch a' Chuillinn and make one $3\frac{1}{2}$-mile tadpole loch of wriggling shape. The controlled River Bran flowing through the lochs is thus used to drive a 2-megawatt turbine. At the Achanalt Falls there is a fish pass to help the salmon reach their spawning ground.

Loch á Chroisg. You motor along the north shore of this loch if you turn off at Achnasheen for Kinloch-ewe, and if the surroundings are a bit bleak there are

Loch Garve, edged by road and railway

glimpses of nobler things in the rocky peaks of Torridon and Coulin thrusting above the rounder hills. Trending east and west for $3\frac{1}{2}$ miles, the maximum breadth is $\frac{1}{2}$ a mile and the maximum depth of 168 ft occurs near the centre. It is a simple basin containing good trout and char. Loch Maree hotel has fishing rights.

Loch Gowan. This irregular sheet of water lies between the Kyle of Lochlash road and the railway line a mile south of Achnasheen, and is really two lochs, separated by alluvial material deposited by the Allt Mhartuin stream. Regarded as one loch, the length is $1\frac{3}{4}$ miles or thereabouts, with the greatest depth in the southern blob at 52 ft, whereas the rather narrower northern basin reaches only 17 ft.

Loch Beannachan. Although there is a footpath to this loch from Loch Gowan and the walk is hardly five miles, the only public road is from Strath Conon following up the Meig into the hills nearly as far as you can go. It is a moorland loch, $1\frac{3}{4}$ miles long by $\frac{1}{3}$ of a mile in maximum breadth and the maximum depth near the centre is 176 ft. The feature of the simple basin is the wooded island where the Meig enters and leaves the loch.

Loch Garve. North-east of Loch Luichart and edged by road and railway, Loch Garve occupies a wooded

hollow under the hulk of Ben Wyvis, so there is the contrast between an oval of water only 220 ft above sea-level under summits rising to over 3,000 ft. Length 1½ miles, maximum breadth ½ a mile, with a maximum depth of 105 ft near the centre, Loch Garve is a simple basin spilling out eastward by Loch na Croic and the Blackwater. The Rogie Falls should be visited, and are easily reached by footpath from a point near Achilty Inn. It is a colourful place in autumn with the white water pouring over the rocky gorge hung with golden birches.

Once upon a time Loch Garve reached to the site of the present falls, and was lowered naturally by the erosion of the glacial drift deposits and the cutting action of the water draining it back. The present loch is 20 ft above the level of the Falls of Rogie.

Man has had to take a hand in the migration of salmon however, and the runs of 4,000 salmon recorded annually in the Blackwater result from the planting of fry by the North of Scotland Hydro-Electric Board who have a large hatchery at Contin nearby. Fish are caught at the outlet of Loch Garve and other places and stripped of their eggs in autumn, to be hatched indoors during the winter and released as fry in spring, or reared to parr and smolt stages.

Beyond Loch Garve in the River Bran there is a permanent floating trap to catch smolts so that they can be taken downstream to other lochs in the Conon Valley and thus minimise predation. Details of the fishing available in these waters are as follows.

Ross & Cromarty

Water	Loch Achonachie, near Contin, and in specific beats of River Conon between Loch Achonachie and Luichart Power Station. Tailrace Pool.
Fish	Salmon, Trout.
Permits	Loch Achonachie Angling Club (D. MacRitchie, Hon. Sec., Scarasdale, Park Road, Strathpeffer).
Charges	From banks—per rod 25p day; £1 week; £1·50 fortnight. Boat—£1 day (2 rods). Fishing on specific beat on Conon £1 day. No Sunday fishing.
Water	Loch Meig near Contin.
Fish	Trout.

Permits	Loch Achonachie Angling Club (D. MacRitchie, Hon. Sec., Scarasdale, Park Road, Strathpeffer).
Charges	From banks – 37½p day; from boat (2 rods) £1 day. No Sunday fishing.

Water	Loch Glascarnoch near Garve.
Fish	Trout.
Permits	Aultguish Inn, By Garve, Ross-shire.
Charges	From banks – 25p day; 75p week; £1·50 month. Hire of boat (2 rods) £1 day.

Water	River Blackwater (Upper Beat) between Loch na Croic outflow and point immediately above Falls of Rogie.
Fish	Salmon.
Permits	Loch Achonachie Angling Club (D. MacRitchie, Hon. Sec., Scarasdale, Park Road, Strathpeffer).
Charges	£1 day. Fly and spinning but no working. No Sunday fishing.

Water	River Conon (part).
Fish	Salmon, Trout.
Permits	Loch Achonachie Angling Club (D. MacRitchie, Hon. Sec., Scarasdale, Park Road, Strathpeffer).
Charges	£1 day on specific beat.

Water	River Conon (New Pool, Morrison Pool and Bridge Pool), Conon Bridge.
Fish	Sea trout.
Permits	Dingwall & District Angling Club (G. Donaldson, Sec., 8 Henderson Crescent, Conon Bridge).
Charges	37½p day; £1 week; £2 month. Fly only. Use of spinning or casting reels prohibited. Breast waders prohibited. No Sunday fishing.

Loch Achilty. Situated near Contin this small deep loch is worth a visit, for although it is only 1,500 yds by 700 yds it is 119 ft deep and contains char. The combination of great depth to size and sheltered position allied to small drainage area result in a remarkable range of water temperature, from 63·5°F.

overleaf: The cleft of the Black Rock of Novar where the outlet of Loch Glass swirls

at the surface to 42·3°F. at 70 ft, a range of 21·2° at its most extreme. Delta gravels relating to the 100-ft beach period show that the Conon has filled in the loch to the west and the Blackwater to the east. The hole the loch occupies was probably dug out by glacier ice before the land rose following the period of glaciation.

Loch Glass and Loch Morie do not belong to the Conon Basin drainage, but because they belong to the Cromarty Firth it is expedient to include them lying as they do just north of Ben Wyvis. Both of them are simple rock basins, sinking to a deep point and rising again. In terms of great volume, they are important lochs.

The approach to Loch Glass is from Evanton to the north of Dingwall, by a narrow track leading in a mile to a strange cleft known as the Black Rock of Novar, a narrow gorge through which the river swirls between twisting puddingstone walls which seem to touch in places. The rock is conglomerate, and adventurous men have forced a way up the river by a combination of rock climbing and inflatable boat. Leave the car and descend to the lip of this impressive ravine if you would see the place. Otherwise follow the track up Glen Glass to the loch in another five miles.

Four miles long and $\frac{2}{3}$ of a mile broad, Loch Glass occupies a sporting hinterland. The road serves shooting lodges sited on its shores. Slightly crescent shaped, and 713 ft above sea-level, the maximum depth is 365 ft with a mean depth of 159 ft. The 300-ft basin runs along the flat bottom for over a mile and the 200-ft basin for 2 miles. A great deal of fluvio-glacial litter bestrews the lower glen, but there is no rock barrier before the Falls of Eillenach.

Loch Morie occupies much lower country than Loch Glass, and has been excavated less deeply, but the character is the same, a narrowish loch among heathery hills. The length here is $2\frac{1}{3}$ miles by just over $\frac{1}{2}$ a mile broad, with a maximum depth of 270 ft and a mean of 125 ft. The outlet stream in this case flows over a barrier of rocks. The best access is from the A836 near Alness.

Lochs of the Torridon Basin
Lochs Damh and Dhugaill

Loch Damh. If you follow up the river which passes under Bridge of Balgy on the fine road from Loch Torridon to Shieldaig you climb in a short distance to Loch Damh, shaped like a boomerang between impressive hills. Take the track on the east side of the Balgy if you intend to walk the shore for any distance, for the west path peters out at the loch, and the deep burn is quite difficult to ford. In fact you can walk right through the hills south to the public road above Loch Kishorn if you have a mind. Better still however is just to climb some of the way up Ben Damh for a bird's eye view of the rather secret loch.

The advantage of climbing is that you see the north-south setting in relation to the high peaks of Liathach and Beinn Alligin stretching west to east across Loch Torridon. Four miles long by $\frac{3}{4}$ of a mile broad, the loch is 206 ft in maximum depth with a mean of 59 ft. The bed is in three basins separated by shallower water. The largest and deepest in the centre of the loch stretches for $2\frac{1}{2}$ miles. The north basin reaches a maximum of only 34 ft, but the southern basin goes down to 135 ft maximum. The fishing for salmon, sea trout, *Salmo ferox* and brown trout is good.

Loch Dhugaill. This little loch lies over the other side of Ben Shieldaig on the public road from Shieldaig to Kishorn and properly belongs to the Applecross peninsula. Situated on the fringes of the most westerly stand of Caledonian pine forest in Scotland, it too contains salmon, sea trout and what I've been told is yellow trout.

Shaped like a narrow triangle pointed north-west the loch is just over $\frac{1}{2}$ a mile long by $\frac{1}{4}$ of a mile broad at the base, but the maximum depth is 108 ft in the middle with a mean of 38 ft.

overleaf: Loch Damh above the Bridge of Balgy

Lochs of the Gairloch Basin

Lochs na Houigh, Vallich, á Ghobhainn, Braigh Horrisdale, Badachro, Bad an Sgalaig

North across Upper Loch Torridon behind the peaks of Beinn Alligin and Beinn Dearg lie the strange lochs of the Flowerdale Forest in the roadless country which stretches to the narrow neck of land between Gairloch and Loch Maree. The easy routes in are from the north side, though the climber will get a better appreciation of the terrain by following in the Coire Mhic Nobuil path from Torridon House and looking down from the top of Beinn Dearg on this rough wing of land entirely fringed by the sea on the west and edged by Loch Maree to the east. Moreover, if it is a day of fine visibility the view from Skye to the Outer Hebrides is the perfect complement to the immediate foreground. I have been lucky on several occasions, in springtime, when the chances of good weather are most favourable.

Loch na h-Oidhche or Loch na Houigh and Loch a Bheallaich or Vallich are the most inaccessible of the lochs, lying on different sides of the 2,869-ft peak of Bus Bheinn. The first named is the higher of the two at 1,250 ft above sea-level and there is a good path to it from a footbridge just east of Loch Bad an Sgalaig on the Gairloch–Loch Maree road. An hour and a half would see you up there in the impressive hollow between steep peaks, Beinn Dearg to the south, and Beinn an Eoin to the east.

The oval loch trending NNW–SSE is $1\frac{3}{4}$ miles long by $\frac{1}{2}$ a mile in maximum breadth and reaches 121 ft in depth near the centre forming on the whole a simple basin.

Loch Vallich lies only a mile or so westward and can be reached in a rough walk round the end of Bus Bheinn, otherwise you must make the long approach from the north-west at Shieldaig near Badachro. Loch Vallich is narrower and lies at a more westerly angle than the first mentioned. The length is the same $1\frac{3}{4}$ miles but the breadth is less than $\frac{1}{2}$ a mile, the mean being $\frac{1}{4}$ of a mile. The depth too is less, 92 ft maximum near the middle western portion.

The loch has three basins in its complex formation, each more than 50 ft deep but separated by shallower water coinciding with constrictions in shape. Half a mile from the west end near the southern shore the

Loch na Houigh (left) under Beinn an Eoin, with Loch Maree and its islands to the right

rocks are covered by only two feet of water.

A short outlet stream no more than 200 yds leads out of Loch Vallich into Loch á Ghobhainn, an elliptical opening only $\frac{3}{4}$ of a mile long by $\frac{1}{3}$ of a mile broad and 28 ft in maximum depth, and the outflow leads to a similar globular water in Loch Gaineamhach. Following down the stream beyond you come to Loch Braigh Horrisdale in four miles. Shallow and roughly triangular in shape the length is $\frac{3}{4}$ of a mile by $\frac{1}{3}$ of a mile in maximum breadth with a greatest depth of 51 ft in the central portion.

Loch Bad a Chroth or Badachro receives the outflow of the above, but the loch is hardly more than an expansion of the river and all of it except 10 per cent is under 10 ft depth, but the maximum is 23 ft. The mean depth of the weedy loch is 6 ft. It is good for salmon and sea trout running up the short distance from the sea.

Loch Bad an Sgalaig. This loch fed from Loch na Houigh, mentioned at the beginning of this section, has been harnessed for electricity with disastrous effects to the Kerrysdale Falls. The impressive cascade is now inside a pipe and the glen is no more than a receptacle for this monstrosity. Such bad taste is not typical of the North of Scotland Hydro-Electric Board whose workings are normally unobtrusive. This is an eyesore running beside the public road replacing a scene of marvellous beauty with ugliness.

The dam at the neck of the glen which contains the water is tiny enough, and its effect has been to join together the Dubh Loch to the south with Loch Bad an Sgalaig in a total length of just over 2 miles by $\frac{1}{2}$ a mile in maximum width. The capacity of the new reservoir is 920,000,000 gallons and the 1,250 kilowatt powerhouse is $\frac{1}{2}$ a mile below the dam.

The Gairloch Angling Club have the fishing rights. There is pike as well as brown trout.

Lochs of the Carron Basin

Lochs Sgamhain and Dhoughaill (Doule)

Leaving Achnasheen and Loch Gowan behind you on the run south-westwards to Kyle of Lochalsh, you pass from the eastward drainage system of the Conon to the western drainage of the Carron, and the first loch of this basin is Loch Sgamhain beneath the 3,000-ft peak of Moruisg. Not a very inspiring country scenically – too much bare foreground and not enough inspiring background, nor is the loch itself of special interest though it is good for salmon, sea trout and char. A mile long by $\frac{1}{3}$ of a mile in maximum width, the maximum depth is 72 ft.

Loch Dhoughaill, or Doule at Achnashellach is more exciting, set beneath the crags of Fuar Toll where Forestry Commission plantings mingle with Caledonian pines in Coire Lair. Good paths lead into the hills on the north side, with cross-country routes to Torridon, over high or low passes as preferred.

The loch itself is 2 miles long by rather less than $\frac{1}{2}$ a mile in maximum breadth, tapering off until it is merely an expansion of the River Carron. The maximum depth of 179 ft occurs near the top end and like Loch Sgamhain there is salmon, sea trout and char. There are long hard ways east across the hills to Loch Monar.

Lochs of the Broom Basin

Because the Conon and the Shin drainage basins encroach so far west, the Loch Broom catchment is small leaving only two lochs to be dealt with, Loch a' Bhraoin to the south and Loch Achall to the east of Ullapool. Loch a' Bhraoin, as mentioned in the Gruinard section, lay on the drove road for cattle driving through the hills by the Strath na Sheallag to the Dirrie More. Over 800 ft above sea-level you merely glimpse it from the Braemore–Dundonnell moorland road, but a lover of lochs should leave his car and walk the mile of track leading down to it.

The setting under the steep front of the Fannich peaks is not unrelieved wildness. Scrubby trees grow among the rocks. Shapely peaks rise to the west, the path along the shore steering for them before twisting north for An Teallach and the bothy of Shenavall–a superlative walk. Happy the man who could be dropped here by car and picked up at Gruinard or Dundonnell. Alternatively you could climb the 3,276 ft peak of A' Chailleach as I did and look over the loch into the great Fionn Loch wilderness, or exchange it by a turn of the head for the Beinn Dearg peaks whose eastern glens lead down to the Kyle of Sutherland.

Loch a' Bhraoin is over $2\frac{1}{2}$ miles long by $\frac{1}{2}$ a mile in maximum breadth and its greatest depth of 73 ft is reached half a mile from the outlet. It is a simple basin with a mean depth of roughly half its maximum. The trout are said to be good. The word Broom is from Bhraoin, meaning the place of rain showers.

Loch Achall is a popular trout and salmon fishing loch 2 miles east of Ullapool with Caledonian pines and mixed woodlands. Although you are so close to the Atlantic, the drainage from the next loch only 5 miles further on is to the North Sea. Loch Achall is just over $1\frac{3}{4}$ miles long by $\frac{1}{2}$ a mile in maximum depth with a greatest depth of 70 ft near the centre. The floor is irregular with shallows among deeper water, at the west end.

The rough grain of Loch Lurgain

Lochs of the Garvie Basin
Lochs Lurgain, Bad a' Ghaill and Owskeich

Garvie Bay is an inlet of Enard Bay, the big inlet to the
south of Lochinver on the Rhu Coigach and the
connected lochs which feed each other are all notable
for salmon and trout. To reach them means going
north out of Ullapool and west at Drumrunie. This is
the road to Achiltibuie and Reiff by Loch Lurgain on
the south edge of the Inverpolly Nature Reserve.
Go all the way to the sea if you would appreciate the
contrasts between the bristling pinnacles of Stac Polly
and the rocky grain of the interior, then the trans-
formation of the green coastal fringe with its white
crofts and cheerful outlook across the Summer Isles to
the big peaks of Ross. The road is narrow and requires
careful use of passing places. Beware of caravans.

Loch Lurgain is 4 miles long and just over ½ a mile in
maximum breadth with heathery and rocky shores,
and is divided into two basins by large islands and
shallow water. The maximum depth is 156 ft with a
mean of 61 ft. Despite being divided it can be regarded
as a true rock basin, even to its outlet.

The east is the deeper basin and is simpler than the
western one which in a central constriction has
shallows with deeper water on both sides. Loch
Lurgain when measured for temperature proved to
have a wider range between top and bottom than any
other loch in this district, no less than 5·8°, with a fall
of 3·4° between 50 and 100 ft.

Loch Bad a' Ghaill. This is another true rock basin
and the length is just over 2 miles by ¾ mile in maximum width, with a mean of ½ mile and a maximum
depth of 180 ft. It is also in two basins, the south-
eastern being deeper and larger.

Loch Owskeich is 1½ miles long by ¾ of a mile in
maximum breadth and is a rock basin in low ground.
There is deep water under the south-eastern shores
which are steep compared to the gentler north-
westerly slopes. The maximum depth is 153 ft and
occurs 300 yds from the eastern shore.

Visitors who are thinking of climbing Stac Polly
should not be put off by its rocky appearance. From
the east ridge it is only a walk, all the pinnacles can
be by-passed and the return journey can be done
easily in two hours. It is worth it for the impression
of the watery maze to the north.

Lochs of the Polly Basin
Lochan Gainmheich and Loch Sionascaig

These two lochs are almost continuous, and the track in from the cairn and Nature Conservancy notice board on Loch Lurgain near Linneraineach cottage offers one of the finest short walks in the Highlands. Its main charm is the vista which opens before you over the low pass as you see the watery maze of the lochs winding over low moor, the feeling of space heightened by monolithic peaks springing up from it, Stac Polly immediately westward, Cul Beag east, and northward Cul Mor and the butt end of Suilven.

Walking this track I met two ladies who said, 'Do you know, you are the first person we have seen for six hours?'. I could have told her of camping for days in here and seeing no one at all, prolonging my stay thanks to the fish I caught. That was in pre-Nature Conservancy days. Now a National Nature Reserve, it is second in size only to the Cairngorms, and it is nearly as uninhabited despite having seashore, marine islands and fresh-water islands within its boundary. No other reserve in the west Highlands offers such scope for research into the factors affecting birch growth and regeneration, of the relic woodlands even if they cover only 3 per cent of 26,827 acres.

Lochan Gainmheich is a short $1\frac{1}{4}$ miles along the path from Loch Lurgain, but if the day is fine it is better to take the right fork of the path and climb up Cul Mor a little to appreciate the uniqueness of the terrain below, where the squiggly shore lines enclose sandy bays, and densely wooded islands contrast with bare moor and pink Torridonian sandstones.

It is easy to drop down to Gleann Laoigh reaching the sandy bay through the sizable wood clinging to the hillside. A harder cross country expedition is to come from the east, leaving the main road at Lochan an Ais and wending round Cul Beag; that is the way I came with my camp kit to put the tent down at Lochan Gainmheich, surprised to see the rigs of former cultivation in this remote spot.

Lochan Gainmheich is almost divided in two by a headland, so has been measured in two portions, the southerly deeper basin, and the shallower northern one. The details are as follows. Southern portion, length 1 mile from east to west, and nearly $\frac{1}{2}$ a mile in maximum breadth, the centrally placed deepest part being 120 ft. The mean is 42 ft.

The northern part is only $\frac{1}{3}$ of a mile long by $\frac{1}{4}$ of a mile with a maximum depth of 59 ft and a mean of $24\frac{1}{2}$ ft. The bottom is more irregular than the southern portion and the outflow is into Loch Sionascaig. By following the north shore of the loch past the fishing bothy you can cross a plank bridge at the outflow and follow the path back to Loch Lurgain.

You would hardly follow the wriggling shore lines of Loch Sionascaig which are so irregular that they cover 17 miles, though the length measured from the south-east end to the north-west arm is 3 miles, and the mean breadth is $\frac{2}{3}$ of a mile. The Bathymetric Survey describes the contour lines of the floor as forming an intricate maze with the maximum depth 216 ft and the mean $60\frac{1}{2}$ ft. There are three main basins:

1 The whole main body of water surrounding the biggest island, Eilean Mor.
2 The north-east arm.
3 The north-west arm.

No. 1 is the largest and the deepest, with two areas exceeding 150 ft, the one to the south of Eilean Mor containing the greatest depth of 216 ft. There are two hills on the bottom to the west of Eilean Mor, the one nearest to the island covered by only 38 ft of water, the other being covered by 41 ft of water.
No. 2 has a maximum depth of 137 ft and is much smaller than No. 1.
No. 3 has a maximum depth of 66 ft and is cut off from the main basin by very shallow water.

These levels are three feet higher than they would be in nature, due to a sluice built to control the outflow of the loch and stabilise the flow of water for angling. It still operates.

The wooded islands are of outstanding botanical interest, Eilean Mor having large birch trees, and rowan almost pure over several acres, but heavy grazing by deer prevents natural regeneration. The island to the north of it is covered with smaller and more scrubby trees, birch, rowan and willow, with two-foot-high holly bushes in places. Black-throated divers breed and it has been established on good

overleaf: Loch Gainmheich (in the foreground) and Loch Sionascaig

Golden eagle chick with prey

The same eaglet 21 days later

authority that the great northern diver bred elsewhere in Western Ross in 1970, while nesting redwings
are no longer regarded as uncommon in this part of
the world.

A list of the breeding birds of Inverpolly gives an
idea of what to expect in this rather sterile type of acid
terrain. The authority is the Nature Conservancy.

Black-throated diver, shag, heron, eider, red-
breasted merganser, buzzard, kestrel, red grouse,
ptarmigan, black grouse, oyster catcher, lapwing,
golden plover, woodcock, common sandpiper, greenshank, greater black-backed gull, lesser black-backed
gull, herring gull, common gull, common tern, arctic
tern, wood pigeon, cuckoo, tawny owl, skylark, raven,
hooded crow, great tit, coal tit, tree creeper, wren,
dipper, ring ouzel, blackbird, wheatear, stonechat,
whinchat, redstart, robin, meadow pipit, rock pipit,
bullfinch, chaffinch, and yellow hammer.

Not a big list, and of course some of the birds
belong to the seaward fringe of the Reserve and the
easiest approach to Loch Sionascaig is from the coast
road to Lochinver, the walk being about half a mile
to where the boats are kept. The fly fishing for brown
trout is good, the average being about $\frac{1}{2}$ lb although
weights of 5 lbs and more are not uncommon. There
is char in the loch also, but no salmon or sea trout due
to an impassable fall. Permits to fish can be obtained
from the Estate Manager's Office at Inverpolly,
telephone Lochinver 252. There is a charge of £1 per
day for each rod, and two boats are available, with
or without ghillie.

The grey rocky knolls of Lewisian gneiss entrapping
little lochans between them makes this north-westerly
point of Ross seem like Sutherland with $8\frac{1}{2}$ per cent of
the land surface water. The reason why it was given
Nature Reserve status was to conserve its great variety
of aquatic, woodland, moorland and mountain
habitats and let them evolve naturally with the
minimum interference by man, yet exercise scientific
control to repair the damage of prolonged misuse by
overburning and overgrazing. The surviving trees
can be taken as relics of a northern type scrub which
once covered the whole region, but now survives only
on the islands and in scattered blocks, some wet, and
some well drained by their steep slopes.

The outflow of Loch Sionascaig by a miniature box
canyon impassable to migratory fish is in contrast to

the mile long sluggish flowing section which ends its short course to the sea. The water, running through peat, is deep and a good lie for salmon and sea trout. An electronic counter records that over 1,800 salmon and a few large sea trout go up annually, 70 per cent of them grilse. The tagging of salmon kelts has resulted in 6 previously spawned fish being recovered in other rivers; 1 from the Gruinard, 2 from the Naver, 1 from the Halladale and 2 from coastal nets, which proves that not all fish return to their home rivers.

Pearl fishing is also done in the middle stretches of the Polly where the mussel is abundant, also in the Allt an Strathain a little to the north. Intending pearl fishers should consult Inverpolly Estates. Tinkers or travelling folk are the main pursuers of this ancient craft.

Mention should also be made of the Lower Polly Loch which is only 200 yds away from the parking places on the Lochinver road. This little loch is at the top of the Polly, and July and August are the best months for salmon and sea trout. There is a boat on the loch and the charge is £1 per day.

Permit holders should consider fishing some of the remoter lochs away from the road, even if it means a walk of a mile or two. These lochs are seldom fished, and for very little trouble the rewards can be high. The Estate Manager at Inverpolly issues a little guide with the permit showing where all the available lochs lie.

There are also hill lochs like Coulin, Adder, Sand, Stack and Loch of the Island which may be fished at 50p for the day, so there is no lack of opportunity in this part of the world. Wandering over this big area it soon becomes clear why this rough ground could never support more than just a few crofters growing barley and potatoes and grazing a few black cattle.

It is interesting to note that the rigs of cultivation in Gleann Laoigh date from after 1758, and it is thought that the folk who dug them were victims of the clearances driven out from the Sutherland straths at the sheep time. This land too came under sheep, but the details of why and where the people went are hidden in vagueness.

The game books of the nineteenth century tell a similar story to that of Osgood Mackenzie, of steady decline in game abundance, due doubtless to destruction of habitat in a fragile environment of high rainfall and basically low productivity. Now we are trying to learn from nature how to put back what we have taken away.

Above Loch Polly, looking across to Suilven and Canisp

Lochs of the Kirkaig Basin

Lochs Borralan, Urigill, Cam Loch, Veyatie, a' Mhiotailt, Fionn Loch

Because Loch Veyatie and the Fionn Loch form the boundary of the Inverpolly National Nature Reserve, Knockan Cliff Visitor Centre at the eastern end is a good place to stop on the run north between Ullapool and Inchnadamph. Here indeed is contrast, where an outcrop of limestone makes an oasis of green in surroundings of bogs and rocks. The Nature Conservancy have made a big effort to interpret the country for you here, with information, explanation and ideas for walks and motor trails. The jargon name for this is 'Interpretative Conservation'.

Knockan is geologically famous since its exposure of old rocks folded over young played an internationally important role in the understanding of structural geology. The explanation of stresses on the earth's crust forcing old rocks over young was deduced hereabouts and with the aid of the Knockan Cliff Geological Nature Trail pamphlet you can glean something of the nature of these cataclysmic forces.

The name given to it here is the Moine Overthrust and it occurred about 400 million years ago during the Caledonian mountain building movements when a wave of schist a hundred miles long came from the east and over-rode the gneiss in a great crumpling and crushing action, forcing the gneiss onto its crest in places. This petrified sea is all about you here, with quartzite of Cambrian age and infinitely older Torridonian sandstone.

The epitome of all this is expressed in the view from the crofts of Elphin looking over the limestone green to the sandstone Matterhorn of Suilven, rearing up over hummocks of gneiss. Impossible to walk in a straight line to it because of the Kirkaig lochs which form the Assynt frontier. The finest guidebook to it is *The Inverpolly Motor Trail*, written to interpret the wild life and scenery of the 50-mile circuit round Suilven by Skiag Bridge, Lochinver and Drumruinie.

Loch Borralan by Altnacealgach Hotel lies furthest to the east in bare peaty ground and is weedy almost everywhere. Length just over 1 mile by $\frac{1}{4}$ of a mile in maximum breadth, the greatest depth is 21 ft. A good

Suilven, the Matterhorn of Scotland, a plinth of pink sandstone on grey gneiss

trout loch, its remarkable feature for a shallow loch is its abundance of char. It decants into the Cam Loch as does Loch Urigill to the south-west.

Loch Urigill like all the other lochs in this basin trends south-east–north-west and it is nearly 2 miles in length with a maximum breadth of $\frac{3}{4}$ of a mile and a maximum depth of 40 ft at the north-west end. Weedy and generally shallow, the mid-loch section is covered by only 3 ft of water. The trout are good.

Cam Loch makes a mirror for the most dramatic view of Suilven, thrusting up in two prongs of sandstone and looking much higher than its 2,399 ft. There is a path along the north side of the loch from Ledbeg, a mile north of the Ledmore junction, but it does not go all the way to the mountain and walking is rough after four miles.

It is a good way to see the Cam Loch which is a shallow rock basin $2\frac{3}{4}$ miles long and $\frac{3}{4}$ of a mile broad, maximum depth 122 ft. Cam, meaning 'crooked', is a true description for a miniature Sionascaig even to islands, one of them large, Eilean na Gartaig by name. Another, Eilean na Gaoithe, has a fin of shingly sand projecting 100 yds from its northern point, the islands being situated at the south-eastern end, which is shallow.

The main basin is north-west where two soundings of 122 ft occur separated by a mile. The north-eastern shore with its little cliffs drops deeply, a sounding of 91 ft being taken only 20 ft from the side. The floor of the loch is composed of Archean rocks in the west, with Torridonian and Cambrian strata in the central and east portions. A wild torrent flows out from it into Loch Veyatie.

Loch Veyatie is only half a mile from Elphin and it has good relics of the northern scrub birch along its southerly shore. It is 4 miles long but less than $\frac{1}{2}$ a mile wide and the maximum depth is 126 ft, with a mean of 41 ft. It is a rock basin, and evidence shows it was once connected to the Fionn Loch, when it would be $7\frac{1}{2}$ miles long, with an offshoot arm where Loch a' Mhiotailt is situated.

Uneven on the floor with a few islands dotted along its shores it is dominated by Cul Mor on one side and Suilven on the other, with little Loch a' Mhiotailt lying between it and Loch Sionascaig.

Loch a' Mhiotailt is just over $\frac{1}{2}$ a mile in length, $\frac{1}{4}$ of a mile in maximum breadth and the maximum depth is 69 ft. Lying at right angles to Loch Veyatie the two lochs become one in heavy rainfall when the rock and sand barrier is covered. I have only looked down on it from the top of Cul Mor and Suilven, for the loch is almost imprisoned in steep hillocks of gneiss.

Fionn Loch lies ¾ of a mile north-west of Veyatie under Suilven. The easiest walk in is from Inverkirkaig following the river past fine waterfalls to the Fionn Loch in 5 miles of good path. Suilven is hardly more than 2,000 ft above you here, and the scramble up between the two peaks by the gully is easy. No rock climbing is involved and there is no better position for appreciating the watery topography of Inverpolly and Assynt.

The evidence that the Fionn Loch was once at a higher level than now can be clearly seen in the alluvial terraces above the loch, the main ones at 20 and 30 ft above the present surface. As can be expected there is considerable irregularity over the length of 2½ miles, the deepest water being in the widest part at 90 ft where the loch is ⅓ of a mile broad. The mean depth is 20½ ft.

The North of Scotland Hydro-Electric Board had the idea of turning the pages of history by building a dam to make Fionn Loch and Loch Veyatie into one long loch and pipe it to a power house on the Kirkaig below the falls ¾ of a mile from the present outlet of the lochs. This would have raised the levels by 44 ft and 52 ft respectively, which would have meant the loss of that woodland of natural scrub along the south bank of Loch Veyatie. The Nature Conservancy rightly opposed the scheme which would have breached a wilderness by roads and massive workings, making nonsense of their management plans.

The scheme was shelved for different reasons however. The estimated revenue on the 14 megawatt generating station was considered to be too low for the capital investment required. Also, new and better methods of generating electricity were coming into being, nuclear and coal fuelled. The wilderness remains for all to enjoy. No roads or footpaths traverse it completely and all the lochs have good trout.

Recommended centres for exploration are Ullapool, Inverkirkaig, Achiltibuie and Lochinver. My own choice would be Achiltibuie for the charm of Rhu Coigach and the views west from the crofts over the Summer Isles to the big peaks of Ross.

Lochs of the Inver Basin

*Lochs Assynt, Leitir Easaich, Maol a' Choire, Awe,
Beannach, Druim Suardalain, na Doire Daraich*

Loch Assynt takes its name from the rockiest parish in
Britain and is the six-mile remnant of a more horse-
shoe shaped loch, before it was silted up by the Loanan
at the top and the cutting back of the Inver at the
bottom where the alluvial terraces are still traceable.
Situated on the Traligill Fault, there are sharp
contrasts between the limestone-rich greens of Inchnadamph beneath grey Ben More, highest peak in
Sutherland, and the sea of gneiss from which protrudes
the eroding tooth of Suilven in an advanced state of
decay. When the pink of sunset glows on this strange
landscape it responds like snow, paling gradually to
bleached bones, leaving only the loch afire. In wind
and rain no other part of Scotland is more inhospitable.
Yet the magic of Assynt is such that you will want to
come back again and again, for it holds so much that is
secret.

It has disappearing streams and potholes linked by
passageways dangerous because of the speed at which
they can flood in an area of 100 in. of rain per annum.
It has caves which have been described as '. . . among
the most interesting archaeological sites in Scotland'.
It has limestone pavements similar to the Burren in
Ireland, rich in arctic-alpine flowers, and with a scrub
vegetation common in Norway but rare in Scotland.
By contrast to this low plateau, the gneiss reaches its
highest elevation in Scotland at over 3,000 ft on Ben
More.

The caves of the Allt nan Uamh 2 miles south of
Loch Assynt have yielded up exciting finds to various
excavators, the bones of red deer, reindeer, brown
bear, northern lynx, badger, otter, northern vole,
arctic lemming and the remains of hundreds of
ptarmigan compared to only a few of those of red
grouse; evidence that Scotland was a more arctic land
when streams began depositing these remains in the
caves.

More recent discoveries include the remains of two
people belonging to the Mesolithic or even Neolithic
period, representing the earliest men in Scotland.
Excavations of other caves nearby are yielding similar
results but more is likely to come to light as digging
goes on. The caves are easily reached by walking for

Loch Assynt and the ruins of Ardvreck Castle

a mile up the south bank of the Allt nan Uamh when you will see them below the north-facing limestone cliff. The connecting channels are dry. The big system of underground passages is higher up with about 1,200 feet of passages.

Behind Inchnadamph Hotel at the top of Loch Assynt the Traligill Burn disappears underground before ending in the loch. Higher up there are more caves and something like 1,500 ft of passages. This is the Cnoc nan Uamh system at 750 ft O.D., and the dry entrance is the 'Cave of the Roaring' – Uamh an Tartair. Going in from here you come to water which plunges down a deep pothole and the 'Cave of the Waterslide' – Uamh an Uisge.

This area is part of the Inchnadamph National Nature Reserve whose boundaries on the north and south are the two streams I have described. Between them lies the undulating limestone plateau with its pavements, sink holes, caves, disappearing streams and willow scrub. Three-quarters of the limestone plateau is composed of an eroding peat cover, where pine trees once grew. The real delight is the flowers. Raven and Walters writing in *Mountain Flowers* (Collins New Naturalist) say,

'There are few botanical centres in Britain more rewarding than Inchnadamph itself, nor any better suited to the indolent. Within a hundred yards of the hotel, on the banks of the Traligill Burn, grow fine clumps of the rare grass *Agropyron donianum*, not to mention an abundance of *Trollius*. Within a quarter of a mile, on the long limestone cliff running southwards, not only purple saxifrage (*S. oppositifolia*) and the *Agropyron* but dark red helleborine (*Epipactis atrorubens*) and the sedge *Carex rupestris* are in unusual plenty. Nearby, in a locality which it is perhaps unwise to define too closely, grows Norwegian sandwort (*Arenaria norvegica*). Barely half a mile to the north of the hotel, on the rabbit-grazed south-facing slopes of a shallow valley, is one of the only two known Scottish stations of *Alchemilla minor*; while on the flat bottom of the valley, which consists of very wet stony patches beside a stream, there grows, amidst a mass of yellow mountain saxifrage (*S. aizoides*), a little of the hair sedge (*Carex capillaris*). Add to this that mountain avens (*Dryas octopetala*) is everywhere abundant, and the attractions of the place should be obvious.'

The attractions are plenty, and there is historical interest as well in the skeletal ruins of Ardvreck Castle on a promontory near the head of the loch – the place where the great Montrose was betrayed for £20,000 and 400 bolls of meal, to be led on horseback through the Highlands to Edinburgh and hanged in the Grassmarket on 21 May 1650, a bitter end for one of the least self-seeking men in Scottish history.

It was the execution of Charles I which brought him out of exile in the Low Countries on behalf of Charles II. He landed in Orkney with the idea of raising the Highlands but shipwreck left him with a feeble army in Caithness for the march south. His first battle was his last, at Carbisdale on the Kyle of Sutherland when his men were cut to pieces by General Strachan's cavalry. Worse still, men whom he had hoped to recruit as allies fought against him.

And he could have done with their local knowledge, for it was a mistake in topography which took him into Strath Oykell and Assynt. Half starved and not knowing where he was, he was glad to meet a Macleod who took him to Ardvreck Castle and what he expected to be friendly shelter.

Instead of that he was clapped in the dungeons while messengers hurried off east to inform General Leslie that they had the wanted man. So the poet, humanitarian, nobleman, covenanter, royalist and soldier-extraordinary was led away to be marched through Scotland tied to a horse.

Macleod had made history too in a special way, for his is the only case of a Highlandman who betrayed a man in need to his enemies for gold. Macleod got his reward, £20,000 in Scots coin, but it turned as sour for him as the balance of meal, for the neighbouring Mackenzies took their revenge for his despicable action by plundering Assynt from end to end, holding it for a hundred years once the Monarchy had been restored and a proclamation of fire and sword made by Charles II against the Macleods.

You can crawl into the dungeons of Ardvreck Castle and see the cannons beneath the stonework. The osprey used to nest on these ruins. There is another memorial which should be visited, at Inchnadamph on a knoll above the loch where the famous geologists B N Peach and J Horne are commemorated for their outstanding work in this classic area. They also uncovered the earliest human evidence of burnt stones, hearths, split bones and sawn reindeer antlers in the Allt nan Uamh caves, together with remnants of prehistoric fauna described earlier in this section, evidence dating back 8,000 years to the Mesolithic era.

The bareness of Loch Assynt is relaxed as you go west along the $6\frac{1}{3}$ miles of its length into lower country with trees and islands to enliven the scene as the shoreline becomes more broken by bays under the fine peaks of Quinag–The Water Stoup. A delightful path crosses low over the west flank to the crofting township of Nedd on the coast road, while a short distance further west is the fault-line of Glen Salach where the narrowing tail end of Loch Assynt makes a sharp dog leg.

Looking at the country it is not surprising to learn that Loch Assynt has an irregular floor of different rock structure, Cambrian and Torridonian at the upper end close to the base of Quinag, while the remainder is Archean gneiss, the whole occupying an ancient consequent valley.

The fishing for trout, sea trout, salmon and salmo ferox is good but the loch has a reputation for being squally. Boats are available at Inchnadamph hotel, and the fishing to non-residents is 50p per day. Char also occurs in the loch. Nearly a mile broad, with a mean breadth of $\frac{1}{2}$ a mile, Loch Assynt attains a maximum depth of 282 ft with a mean of 101 ft, its area being nearly 2,000 acres. There are four areas exceeding 200 ft, the deepest hole being north of Eilean Assynt. The numerous bays are deep.

Loch Leitir Easaich. This small loch at the entrance to Glen Salach and separated from Loch Assynt by only a few yards of streams was originally a part of the larger loch before its level was lowered by natural means. Now they are separated by a fine waterfall, but the rock basin has only 4 per cent covered by more than 50 ft of water in a maximum length of just over $\frac{1}{2}$ mile by $\frac{2}{5}$ mile, with a maximum depth of 70 ft. The fishing is salmon and brown trout and permit arrangements are the same as for Loch Assynt. The local name for the loch is Letteressie and its main feature of interest is its irregularity of outline.

Loch Maol a' Choire is at the Inchnadamph end of the loch and lies inside the Nature Reserve though there is a boat on it and the hotel has the fishing rights. The walk to it by footpath up the Traligill Valley is very fine and fishermen call it the Gillaroo Loch, because, say the Nature Conservancy, '. . . of the alleged resemblance of its trout to the so-called Gillaroo trout of Loughs Neagh and Melcin and the Galway Lakes, in Ireland'. None of these distinctive fishes appears to have been caught for a very long time, possibly because of stocking with trout from other sources. The Gillaroos here had apparently reddish fins but no red spots. Plaster casts of specimens may be seen in the hotel, and the opinion of experts is that the high alkalinity of the water and the abundance of molluscs is reminiscent of the Irish environment.

This hill loch is 600 yds long by 250 yds broad and the maximum depth is 8 ft. South of the loch in the cave pool of the Allt nan Uamh has been found a rare survivor of the Ice Age, the collembolid *Onychiurus schoetti*.

Loch Awe. This small loch, only 7 ft deep and much overgrown, lies just off the road 4 miles south of Inchnadamph, but it is a good salmon loch and fishing arrangements are as for the other lochs. The length is 1,400 yds by 530 yds, and the mean depth is 5 ft.

Loch Beannach. You find this loch north of the stream of the Inver, 2 miles west of Loch Assynt, a fine sinuous loch with wooded islands on a hinterland dotted with lochs stretching all the way to Rhu Stoer and round to Nedd, miles of nothing but watery maze. Beannach is a shallow rock basin in Archaen gneiss $1\frac{3}{4}$ miles long by $\frac{1}{3}$ of a mile in maximum breadth with a maximum depth of 38 ft in its south-westerly portion.

Loch Druim Suardalain is another small rock basin, one of a chain in an ancient valley, length $\frac{3}{4}$ of a mile by $\frac{1}{4}$ of a mile with a maximum depth of 31 ft and a mean depth of only 10 ft.

Loch na Doire Daraich. The other name for this is Loch Culag and fishing is available from Culag Hotel at 75p per day, sea trout and brown trout. Lying close to the village of Lochinver, the length is $\frac{1}{2}$ a mile by $\frac{1}{4}$ of a mile, with a mean depth of only $3\frac{1}{2}$ ft and a maximum of 9 ft.

Anglers coming to this district would be well advised to join the Assynt Angling Club for the right to fish over 30 lochs in Assynt, at a cost of 25p per day, 50p per week or £1 per month; boats 50p. Details can be had from the Commercial Bank, Lochinver, telephone Lochinver 215.

Visitors to the Inchnadamph Nature Reserve should obtain permission from the Assynt Estate Office, Lochinver, telephone Lochinver 203 for any visit between 15 July and 15 October, and for visits by parties of more than six at any time of the year. Research workers from museums and universities are encouraged.

Climbers interested in Suilven will find a good track leading into the hills just north of Loch Culag. The mountain has the hump of a huge haystack from this angle with many verticalities. The easy way is to keep walking until the whole ridge comes into view, then strike up the easy ground between the peaks. It makes a superb and not too strenuous expedition of about 12 miles return journey plus 2,399 ft of ascent.

Walkers should consider making one rather special expedition which has to do with lochs only in passing. It is to the Eas Coul Aulin–The Maiden's Tresses– waterfall which drops from a western spur of the Ben More Assynt range into the head of Loch Glencoul.

The first plunge of the Eas Coul Aulin waterfall which drops 600 ft

The fall is over 600 ft, and the 'tresses' are where the white column of water splits into two before dividing again into many strands on the dark rocks.

I went to it from Loch Ganvich on the summit of the Inchnadamph–Kylesku road, on a rocky path going eastward to the summit of the Bealach a' Bhurich, high enough to be a fine viewpoint for the wild peaks on both sides. Nor shall I forget the little lochan beneath the pass where sandpipers were flitting and a ring ouzel was sending out its thin cry, mournful as a wader.

The point to remember is not to contour too far to the south-west as you go down. Better to strike off at the first burn by a series of heathery steps on the steepening mountainside. In a short distance you come to a lip of bare rock and the sight of the sparkling water making a rainbow mist against the blue sea-loch far below. On this open hillside the whole atmosphere is of light and brightness, the green glen below adding to that impression.

Go in the sunshine after wind and rain and you won't be disappointed. Lacking big drainage it can drop to a trickle in drought. Nevertheless the walk should not be missed. Allow three hours for the return journey. Reflect too that the Eas Coul Aulin which debouches so close to the sea, is yet within only 3 miles of the easterly drainage by the Gorm Loch Mor and the Cassley, a striking example of the short west coast rivers in relation to those flowing east from the watersheds.

We go next to the route Montrose should have taken from Carbisdale, north by the Shin drainage which penetrates into the wild Reay country by a chain of lochs running from north-west to south-east.

Loch Shin since hydro-electrification

Little Loch Shin and part of Lairg village

Lochs of the Shin Basin

*Lochs Shin, a' Ghriama, Merkland, Fiodhaig, Gorm Loch
Mor, Ailsh, Craggie, an Daimh, Migdale, an Lagain, Buidhe*

Lairg on the railway is the hub of the mail bus service
serving the long straths which lead to the west and
north, with connections to such destinations as Bettyhill, Tongue, Durness, Scourie and Lochinver. This
is the country where Norse names mix and conjoin
with Gaelic. Suilven is an example: Sul is the Norse
for Pillar, but Bheinn is the Gaelic for mountain,
with 'ben' its shortened form. Sutherland itself comes
from the Norse Sudrland, meaning the Southern
Land, which it was to the Vikings.

This is the emptiest part of Britain today, as anyone
who travels the long Sutherland straths to the coast
will discover. This is the classic ground of the clearances, where crofters were dispossessed from the best
land to make way for sheep and burned out if they
resisted. The dates 1814 to 1819 are bitterly remembered in Sutherland as evicted men crossed the
Atlantic in overcrowded emigrant ships to try a new
life in Canada or tried to eke out a living on the rocky
coast. The decline in fertility was rapid due to overgrazing by sheep and overburning to promote grazing
growth.

The decline continues, and at 13,000 the population
of Sutherland is roughly half what it was in 1951.
Sheep farming, sporting estates and forestry, with a
seasonal income from tourism, do not disguise the
Highland problem in remote areas like this where
every commodity costs more to an ageing and scattered
community. A twentieth century standard of living
is hard to obtain in Sutherland, yet Lairg has an air
of prosperity about it at the junction of the green
straths by a hydro-electric dam. See it at the big lamb
sales and you realise the enormous amount of mutton
which comes off the hills and glens that in clan times
nurtured cattle. The hundreds of lorries needed to
carry them away tell their own story in destinations
from all over Scotland and much of northern England.

Loch Shin, since hydro-electrification, is the fourth
biggest loch in Scotland and has jostled Loch Shiel
from that position into fifth place. Narrow and bleak
for much of its 17·8 miles it needs the colour of sunset
on clouds and hills to be beautiful. Forestry is
improving it in places and the views out to Ben More

Assynt are fine, but the main attraction of this sheet of water is to anglers. The trout are good, and the Lairg Angling Club supply permits at 25p per day, with boats at 50p for half-day use. There is also a Club Hut at the lochside beyond the Lairg Dam where permits and boats can be obtained.

The narrowness of Loch Shin relative to its length makes it akin to Loch Shiel, but the mean breadth is no longer 3 per cent of the length due to the hydro-electric alterations and capture of the headwaters of the rivers Cassley, Brora and other streams. The mean breadth now is 0·7 miles and the maximum 1·3 miles opposite Fiag Bridge. The raise of level was 37 ft, which would make the greatest depth 199 ft, though half the irregular bottom is covered by less than 100 ft.

Hydro-electrification begins at the top western end of the loch where the Cassley, whose natural flow is into Strath Oykell, is diverted by aqueducts to power a small power station before being tunnelled $2\frac{1}{2}$ miles to a main power station on the west shore of Loch Shin. Electricity generated here is carried to the Durness region, the output being 10 megawatts.

Loch Shin itself has a storage capacity of 64·4 million units of electricity contained behind a dam 1,400 ft long and 40 ft high. A mile below the dam there is another dam, and the water contained between them is known as Little Loch Shin, the lower dam being known as the Shin diversion weir. A power station at the outlet of the top dam provides the local electricity supply.

Fish lifts in both dams enable salmon to enter or leave both lochs, or they can be trapped and stripped of their eggs and milt for artificial rearing in the hatchery for subsequent release in tributaries of the Shin. Compensation water to maintain the flow in the river is passed through a small tubular turbine, but the main station is 5 miles down at Iveran.

A 5-mile-long tunnel leads the water down to a concrete-lined shaft 200 ft deep and 45 ft in diameter, feeding into a steel-lined pressure tunnel 1,700 ft long and $13\frac{1}{2}$ ft in diameter ending in twin 9-ft-diameter steel pipes. The Shin station is of Tarradale stone and discharges the water after use through a 1,900-ft open-channel tail race, with an electric screen at its outlet to prevent salmon from entering. The capacity is 12 megawatts.

Group control of all the Shin valley stations is maintained here by power line carrier telephone from Shin to Cassley and Lairg switching stations. A submarine cable crossing Loch Shin for part of the way leads to Cassley. Power from the main station at Shin connects to Beauly in Ross-shire and Mybster in Caithness.

Canoeists can have fun by paddling up Loch Shin and turning north at Loch a' Ghriama and reaching Loch Merkland in about 2 miles of portaging and continuing north-west after crossing the watershed into the Laxford system. A few adventurers do it, and there can be few more worthwhile ways of enjoying a journey of increasing interest as the peaks of Reay draw nearer.

Loch a' Ghriama can be regarded now as the northerly tip of Loch Shin, length in its own right $1\frac{1}{2}$ miles, breadth just over $\frac{1}{3}$ mile and maximum depth in the centre 64 ft. The brown trout fishing is free to visitors staying in Overscaig Hotel.

Merkland is a narrow ribbon like Shin but has much more character, due to its steeper shores and closing hills, an easy place to watch black-throated divers and listen to their wailing cries. The length is 3 miles but the mean breadth is just $\frac{1}{4}$ of a mile and the maximum a little over $\frac{1}{3}$ of a mile. The maximum depth close to the narrows at the head of the loch is 85 ft and there is an interesting example of the build up of alluvium from burns entering from opposite sides and raising the bottom by their debris. The cone of the Allt nan Albannach on the north-east is smaller than the one laid down by the Garbh Allt to make a shoaling where the depth is only 31 ft, with deep water on both sides of the alluvium. Overscaig Hotel has the brown trout fishing.

Loch Fiodhaig, or Fiag, is a hill loch most easily reached from Loch Shin by following up the stream from Fiag Bridge. It is a good moorland trout loch with islands. The length is $1\frac{1}{2}$ miles and the maximum breadth is $\frac{2}{3}$ of a mile. The maximum depth is 71 ft and the mean depth is 26 ft.

Gorm Loch Mor. Apart from Loch Shin this mile-long sheet of water on the high plateau east of Ben More Assynt has the distinction of being the deepest in the basin with a maximum sounding of 91 ft. Irregular, and with many islands the maximum width is just over $\frac{1}{2}$ a mile, though the mean is less than half of that. The streams which feed it are only 3 miles or so from the Atlantic, yet they drain eastward. The loch itself lies relatively close to the big waterfall of the Eas Coul Aulin mentioned in the last section.

The Gorm Loch Mor is a true rock basin in mainly Cambrian quartzite with evidence of glaciation all around it, relics of the times when the ice from Ben More overflowed over this ground into Loch Shin. The islands on the Gorm Loch Mor are themselves moraines – a place to visit for those who are willing to to make an effort to get to a wild and remote place.

Loch Ailsh is on the River Oykell whose strath running due west from the Shin Power Station has been described as the most beautiful in the Highlands and was the route followed by the ill-fated Montrose. A track branches north-east to the loch just 2 miles south of Altnacealgach Hotel. This is a trout loch with occasional salmon and it is shallow, being no more than 24 ft in maximum depth in a length of just under 1 mile by $\frac{1}{2}$ a mile in breadth. The Oykell flows through it and it lies wholly within a sporting estate.

Loch Craggie. Lies 3 miles south of the above, on the Strath Oykell road and is a true rock basin despite being only $\frac{2}{3}$ mile in length, less than $\frac{1}{5}$ mile broad and 40 ft in maximum depth.

Loch an Daimh. Situated between Ullapool and Oykell Bridge it lies close to the watershed and in the natural course of events will be diverted towards the Atlantic by the cutting action of the Rhidorroch River. Narrow and attractively wooded on the south-east, it makes a fine foreground for the wild peaks of Seana Braigh and the Ben Dearg range which are the highest mountains north of the Grave–Ullapool road.

The loch occupies a fault dislocation and is $1\frac{3}{4}$ miles in length, $\frac{1}{5}$ of a mile in maximum width and is 52 ft at maximum depth in the centre. The conformation is simple. The trout fishing is good. A cross country walker should be tempted by the overnight accommodation which can be found at either end of this route, at Ullapool and Oykell Bridge with 15 miles of good tracks between.

Loch Migdale is about a mile from Bonar Bridge on the Dornoch Firth and is 2 miles long by $\frac{1}{2}$ a mile broad, the greatest depth being 49 ft and the mean 21 ft. The island at the west end is artificial and there is a passageway to it covered by only shallow water. Burghfield House Hotel, Dornoch, has the brown trout fishing which costs with a boat £1·50 per day. Pike also occur in the loch.

Loch an Lagain. A small loch, length 1 mile by $\frac{1}{4}$ of a mile, only 18 ft in maximum depth, lying $3\frac{1}{2}$ miles north-east of Bonar Bridge.

Loch Buidhe lies 5 miles north-east of Bonar Bridge on the Strath Carnoch road to Golspie, and Burghfield House Hotel have the salmon and brown trout fishing, price £1·50p per day including boat. I do not know what the salmon fishing is like, but earlier attempts to introduce salmon failed, according to the Bathymetrical Survey, Volume II. The length of the loch is $1\frac{1}{4}$ miles by just under $\frac{1}{4}$ of a mile width, the maximum depth of 36 ft occurring near the centre.

Lochs of the Laxford Basin

Lochs More, Loch nan Ealachan, Stack, na Cláise Fearna, nam Bhreac

The Laxford drainage begins just over the watershed from Loch Merkland on the Shin. The distance separating the east and west drainage is only 2 miles, but at Loch More there is an immediate change of scenic contrast, the loch is wider, the shores steeper, natural woodlands cling to the gullies and above everything are the near peaks of pointed Ben Stack and the grey head of Arkle, a great bump of Cambrian quartzite.

Yet Loch More, fine as it is, merely introduces better things to come. It is too uniform to be really exciting, with straight shores for its 4 miles of length and an unvarying width of $\frac{1}{2}$ a mile. Dropping to 316 ft deep in the centre the conformation could hardly be simpler.

Loch nan Ealachan is the name given to the shallows of the top end, which are separated from the main loch by stepping stones, the maximum depth inside the subcircular basin being no more than 8 ft with a mean of just under 5 ft.

Loch Stack is the gem of the basin and may well be the finest trout, salmon and sea trout loch in Scotland. Add ferox and char to that, plus a range of wild life that includes pine marten, otter, greenshank, black-throated diver, golden eagle, peregrine falcon and some of the finest red deer in Scotland, then look at the rocks and hanging birches hemming you in and you have the epitome of wildest Sutherland – a mixture of savagery and charm.

I have walked all over this country by the paths which cross to Loch Eriboll or into Strath Dionard and by Glen Golly to Strathmore. But my first-ever-view of Loch Stack remains vivid as I came from the east by the Bealach na Feithe in a wild thunderstorm. Crouched under my cape above hidden Loch Stack waiting for the battering rain and hail to let up, I remember the blurred landscape that began to emerge out of blackness, a confusion of knolls dotting a watery maze, hundreds of them stretching as far as the eye could reach in the territory between Loch Stack and the sea known as Druim na h-Aimnhe. And

Loch More and Ben Stack

it was in this region I met the only pair of red-necked phalaropes I have encountered in the breeding season on the Scottish mainland.

Sutherland does not give up its secrets lightly. The road goes along the south side of Loch Stack but no road goes round it past the keeper's house at Aird-chuilian. Walk from there up the paths which climb the hills east, or go up Ben Stack if you would appreciate the setting. Or you can fish from a boat, at a price, by applying to Cape Wrath Hotel or Scourie or to Westminster Estates. Even without a fish, a day in a boat is worth while here.

The long side of Loch Stack adjoining the public road is 2½ miles and should be regarded as a long stroke of a rough letter H, with a shorter parallel under the grey bulk of Arkle. These two strokes form separate basins joined by no more than a shallow bar of water. Loch Stack is almost two lochs, the greatest depth of 108 ft being in the basin nearest to the road, one mile from the southern end. North-east under Arkle the top basin goes down to 85 ft, but the constriction between the two basins is covered by no more than 16 ft of water.

The big run of salmon occurs in summer, entering from the Laxford River, lax being the Norse word for salmon. The Royal Family sometimes fish here as guests at Loch Stack Lodge, sharing the loch with black-throated divers who are also honoured guests here, and protected against egg thieves.

Loch na Cláise Fearna is on the west road from Laxford Bridge *en route* to Scourie. A wriggly little loch only 38 ft deep with a large central island, the general shape is triangular with a narrow apex pointing north-east.

Loch nam Bhreac. Lies north-west of the last named just off the narrow road that goes to the remote crofting settlement of Foindlemore and not far from Tarbert. A loch which seems to be all arms and promontories with many islands; it is over a mile in maximum length and breadth variable over its 142 acres. The south portion is the widest and it contains the maximum depth of 71 ft, the mean being 28 ft. South-west of the large wooded island the depth is 66 ft, though 54 per cent is covered by less than 25 ft.

A stag in velvet by Loch Stack

Loch Stack

Glassing deer above Loch nan Ealachan

Birds of the Handa and Sutherland coast

Crofts of Foindlemore with Handa Island on the left

No one who gets this far should miss the chance of crossing over to Handa Island from Tarbert. Being an RSPB reserve the boatman is accustomed to taking parties over to the large grassy island whose cliffs are amongst the most spectacular in Scotland for seabirds, puffins, razorbills, guillemots and fulmars. The great feature is the Stack of Handa which thrusts up in pink Torridonian sandstone crammed with birds right to the top. So you can stand on a headland level with its top and look at the clamouring birds only a short distance away with the sea plunging between.

There are lochs on the peaty top of the island, beloved of red-throated divers and frequented by great skuas. The views up the coast are good, with the flanking peaks of Reay stretching a grey line in the direction of Cape Wrath. Handa can also be reached from Scourie, whose lochs we examine next.

Scourie, showing Loch a' Bhaid Daraich

Lochs of the Scourie Basin
Loch an Laig Aird and Loch a' Bhaid Daraich

Scourie situated on greensward on hillocks above a sweep of bay is one of the most attractive places in north-west Scotland, its agricultural impact being all the greater for the rocks and bogs which lead to largish walled fields. The hotel has the fishing of some 280 lochs, five of them with salmon and sea trout, free to hotel guests. Fishing in Loch More and Loch Stack can be arranged. In this rocky world of lochs you hardly expect to find palm trees growing in the open, but they are here, proof of the mildness of this coast. They may be the most northerly palms in the world.

I have chosen to describe only two contrasting lochs which are typical of many. Loch an Laig Aird is a shallow irregular loch covering 67 acres with islands and a projecting promontory. The deepest sounding of 42 ft is south-west of this promontory near the shore. Of the remainder three-quarters of the loch is covered by less than 20 ft.

Loch a' Bhaid Daraich lies almost in the village and has attractive natural birch woods good for birds. A mile long and over one-third of a mile broad it is 121 ft deep in the centre, with a mean depth of $55\frac{1}{2}$ ft. The basin is flat bottomed and simple beneath good rock bluffs north and south.

Walkers who would like more intimate contact with this lochan studded landscape should consider walking the footpath from Duartmore Bridge to Loch Stack Lodge, a distance of seven miles. The daily mail bus would take them back to Scourie, or a return journey could be made by cutting down Strath Stack and hitting off a parallel footpath high above Loch an Leathaid Bhuain.

The tremendous roughness of this hinterland to the south of the Scourie–Laxford Bridge road has to be seen to be appreciated, bosses of gneiss imprisoning lochs each so planed by the passage of ice that the whole landscape has a scalped appearance. And on Eddrachillis Bay there is the same lumpy impression in the black islets where there is said to be one for every day of the year. The probability is that no one has ever visited every loch in this neighbourhood, for it would be a daunting task. I have merely taken a slice of the cake to show the flavour.

Lochs of the Hope Basin
Loch Hope

Look at the map of the flattish top of Scotland and you will notice three bites out of it towards Cape Wrath. The deepest is Loch Eriboll, with the Kyle of Durness to the west and the Kyle of Tongue to the east. Loch Hope must have been a fourth bite when the sea-level was higher, as raised beaches near its head and foot show. Even today the highest tides reach within a $\frac{1}{2}$ mile of Loch Hope and in distant times must have lapped Ben Hope.

Standing at the outlet you are only 12 feet above sea-level, and the river emerging has only a mile to go to reach the sea; small wonder it is so good for salmon and sea trout. Loch Hope means 'The Loch of the Bay of the Harbour', a perfect description of its connection with Loch Eriboll, where King Haco anchored his fleet in the year 1263 and saw an October eclipse of the sun which filled him with foreboding. The feeling of ill omen proved true immediately when men he sent ashore were slain by waiting Picts, though it was a trifle in the events which culminated in the Battle of Largs when the elements again played a vital part in the final Viking defeat.

Strange that history should repeat itself 670 years later when other warships assembled at Loch Eriboll, our own this time, to convoy supply ships in the Battle of the Atlantic when Britain was fighting for survival. Unlike the Vikings we did not lose, though the struggle was close at times.

This is Mackay country, and none of that clan is more real than Rob Donn 'the Bard of Sutherland' who lived near the top end of Loch Hope and has been called the Robert Burns of the North. He died in 1777, a Jacobite at heart though his clan fought on the Hanoverian side. Little good did it do them since Mackay sold the clan lands to the Earl of Sutherland who ordered the clearances in order to get higher rents from the invading flock-masters with their sheep. What scathing poetry Donn could have written of the inhumanities which were to empty the glens he loved!

The road that runs south down the east shore of Loch Hope passes the ruins of a drystone tower called Dun Dornadilla near where Rob Donn was born. The

Loch Hope and Ben Hope, from the northerly outlet

Cliffs of Whiten Head seen across Loch Eriboll (above)

The outlet from Loch Hope (below)

name Dornadilla is said to be taken from a Princess of the pre-Christian era. It is a good landmark for climbing Ben Hope by the Allt na Caillich Burn, which has considerable geological interest in the folded strata which show the layers of succession unusually clearly.

Look out for the alluvial terraces which are the remains of the 50-ft and 100-ft beach deposits. Just over 6 miles long, the maximum width of Loch Hope is $\frac{3}{4}$ of a mile with a greatest depth of 187 ft mid-way along its length. The floor is of uneven Lewisian gneiss and deformed schistose rocks with quartzite at the outlet.

Fishing for trout, salmon and sea trout is not absolutely private but can be arranged from Overscaig, Altnaharra, Bettyhill and Durness hotels at a price of around £5–£8 for two rods and boat with ghillie. Unauthorised fishing is also done by the common seal who take advantage of the short river to hunt in what is almost an extension of the sea. Loch Hope fluctuates to such an extent that between high water in flood and low in drought there is a difference of as much as 11 ft.

The surveyors who sounded the loch mention seeing the reputed remains of an old castle just above the surface of the water about a mile from the outlet and towards the eastern shore. There is a shallow here, with boulders to the west of it, but nothing seems to be known of the castle or its builders. Despite the uneven floor the mean depth for Loch Hope is high at $61\frac{1}{2}$ ft. Only 45 lochs in Scotland have a higher mean, and in length it is 21st. Loch Assynt and Loch Naver exceed in the latter respect.

It is eastward we go now by motoring down Loch Hope and swinging north again from Altnaharra, though wise is the person who would take a little time to leave the car and take a walk up Glen Golly about whose trees Rob Donn wrote a lovely song. When I was there the keeper showed me a very old iron pot he had found one day in that glen. He seemed to treasure it, and had given it a nickname, 'Rob Donn's porridge pot'.

A keen walker can go up the Golly and over a pass to Loch Dionard, one of the most exciting places in Sutherland where a thousand feet of crag spouting waterfalls ends in the bouldery loch. Rock climbers will find superb quartzite here in a setting of infinite solitude, and days I spent here while making the first big routes on this face are amongst the brightest spots in my memory.

Other ways from Strathmore are across the hills from Gobernuisgach to Loch Stack on a fine footpath through the Reay peaks. The fit man who travels light and depends on finding bed and breakfast where he can will find great reward going cross country in Sutherland.

Lochs of the Kinloch Basin
Lochs Chalum and Loch an Dithreibh (Deerie)

These lochs lie in the remote country between Loch Loyal and Loch Hope and I chose to go to them by walking from a house marked Inchkinloch on the A836 Tongue road over the shoulder of Ben Loyal. And I carried lightweight camping equipment, for I had the feeling that Loch an Deerie would prove to have an exceptional setting hemmed by two of the finest peaks in Sutherland. I was right, though I nearly stuck in the wet bogs of Loch Chalum water-logged after continuous heavy rain. The sun was shining now on waving bog cotton and the loch was a patch of irregular blue crinkling beneath the over-topping granite spire of Loyal.

Weedy and with one large island in the middle, Loch Chalum is recognisably a shallow loch, the greater part of it being less than 10 ft deep. Measured from the south-west to the north-east it is $\frac{3}{4}$ of a mile long with a maximum breadth of $\frac{1}{2}$ a mile, with a greatest depth of 30 ft in the western portion. Loch an Deerie into which it drains by a deep burn is a much more exciting proposition, and that evening as I dropped down to it the surface held the yellows and reds of the sunset sky.

No loch I have camped beside has greater character than this one, with golden whins and birches beneath steep bouldery slopes with the drumming of snipe and the wailing of divers adding authentic notes. I climbed Ben Hope and Ben Loyal from here, enjoying warm sun between thunder showers, sometimes in a welter of black clouds and stinging hail, other times looking over moorlands glittering with peat hags to the yellow sands of the Kyle of Tongue only 3 miles distant.

The loch is $1\frac{1}{2}$ miles long and is a uniform width of $\frac{2}{3}$ of a mile with a narrower arm crooking to the north-east. It is deep, with a mean of 66 ft and a maximum in the centre of 157 ft. It is a true rock basin in gneiss, which is exposed on the great crag on its east side. Between the crook of the north-eastern arm and the main basin there is a rise in bottom which gives a sounding of 49 ft deepening again to give a maximum of 59 ft to the smaller basin. Under the east face of Ben Hope lie many attractive lochans.

Lochs of the Borgie Basin
Lochs Coulside, Loyal, and Creagach

Loch Coulside lies close to the house of Inchkinloch mentioned in the last section and drains into Loch Loyal by a mile of river. A mile long by only 250 yds broad the maximum depth is only 14 ft with a mean of $7\frac{1}{2}$ ft.

Loch Loyal with the road running along its west shore under a striking peak has been perfectly described as being like a Wellington boot with the toe pointing west and the leg north. The length is $4\frac{1}{2}$ miles, with a maximum breadth of nearly a mile and a maximum depth of 217 ft. There are two deep basins separated by shallows about $2\frac{1}{2}$ miles from the foot of the loch. The northern one contains the maximum depth, while the top basin reaches 137 ft. Altnaharra Hotel has salmon and trout fishing rights, the latter at 50p per day with boat.

Loch Creagach (Craggie). Only a short stream separates this loch from Loyal and they must have been joined at one time; the barrier between is a mixture of morainic material and alluvium deposited

Loch Loyal, looking north-east

by the stream. A terrace above the lochs points to their one-time continuity. The rock formation is mainly granite.

Length $1\frac{1}{2}$ miles by $\frac{1}{2}$ a mile, it resembles Loch Loyal in that there are two basins separated by shallow water, the deeper being the southern portion which has a maximum depth of 84 ft. The top end where the Borgie emerges is known as Loch Slain. The pleasant village of Tongue is only a short distance away, and near it is a small loch where a cow once picked up a French gold piece, a relic of the time when a French ship bringing money to assist the Jacobites foundered. The men escaped and were rounded up but the gold was never found. The cow seems to prove the story that it was thrown into the loch and later recovered by somebody local—all but an odd gold piece or two perhaps.

Lochs of the Naver Basin

Lochs Naver, na Meide, a' Bhealaich, Choire, Syre

The Naver is an emotive word in Sutherland for the 17-mile-long Strath where the river winds through low-lying country to the sea was the scene of some of the worst evictions. Here on the alluvial flats the crofters had good grazing and land that would yield crops, just the kind of land that could be let at a high price to the profit of the Earl of Sutherland if he could get rid of the crofters. So the people were driven and burned out of their homes and resettled on the infertile coast, and these are the dead and dying townships you will see today if you take the coast road along the north and west tip of Scotland.

The best eyewitness accounts are by the Revd Donald Sage in *Memorabilia Domestica* and the Revd Donald MacLeod in *Gloomy Memories*. MacLeod watched 250 houses going up in smoke at one time. If Rob Donn the bard had been alive he would have immortalised these times, and known how right he was to support the Jacobite cause in songs if not in deeds. The men who had given their service to the Hanoverians had no cause to be proud of it.

You can see the ruins of two of these villages cleared at the beginning of the nineteenth century on the north and south shores of Loch Naver, Reidhachaisteil and Ruighnasealbhaig respectively. The fertile land must have attracted the earliest settlers for there are ruins of Pictish towers and the remains of crannogs, artificial islands used as lake dwellings.

Altnaharra at the west end of the loch is the metropolis today, just a hotel and a cluster of estate houses beneath Ben Klibreck, green hulk of a mountain which has the merit of being a Munro, 3,145 ft. A fine way to climb it is to take the mail bus to Crask Inn and traverse over the top back to Altnaharra. The Klibreck Burn offers a nice easy descent.

Loch Naver is 6 miles long by $\frac{2}{3}$ of a mile broad with a maximum depth of 108 ft in the widest part a mile from the west end. The mean is 39 ft on an irregular floor. Fishing for salmon, trout and sea trout can be arranged at Altnaharra, Bettyhill and Garvault Hotel, Kinbrace.

Loch na Meide is on the Loch Hope–Altnaharra road about 10 miles south of Tongue and its $3\frac{1}{3}$ miles is almost halved by a constriction in the middle. Over

a mile wide at the southern end where it is deepest, maximum 63 ft, it is a true rock basin in Moine schists scooped out by ice radiating from the Ben Loyal and Ben Hope ice cauldron. Irregular in outline with little islands in the southern part the constriction which divides it is covered by only 2 ft of water.

Loch a' Bhealaich and Loch Choire. These two interesting lochs lie parallel to Loch Naver on the other side of Ben Klibreck and, separated by only 200 yds of stream, can be regarded as remnants of one continuous loch. The height difference between them is only 2 ft, and the deepest water of both lochs is nearest to their point of separation. The total length of the two is $4\frac{3}{4}$ miles of which Loch a' Bhealaich forms over $1\frac{1}{2}$ miles with a maximum depth of 80 ft. The maximum breadth is only $\frac{1}{4}$ mile, and the enclosed effect of the steep ground hemming it in is of a corrie loch.

Loch Choire is twice the length and breadth and nearly twice as deep at 151 ft. Tracks lead in from the west near Crask Inn, but from the east there is a road leading off the B871 to the shooting lodge at the wooded north-eastern end of Loch Choire.

Loch Syre. This small loch lies to the north of Loch Naver and has some little islands on its shallow water. The length is $\frac{3}{4}$ of a mile with a maximum breadth of just over $\frac{1}{2}$ a mile. The maximum depth is 12 ft and the mean $5\frac{1}{2}$ ft. The Naver should be followed down to the sea from this point for some exploration of the coast west of Bettyhill where at the end of minor branch roads are some of the remotest crofting communities in Scotland.

Take a look at the crofts of Farr, Sworldly, Kirtomy, Armadale, then go west to Lamigo Bay if you would have a grasp of social history. Look at Skerray where the tiny fields virtually hang on the steep little hills beneath white dots of houses and you will feel the strips of green and yellow cultivation raising your spirits.

Look out to sea over the narrow Kyle of Rannoch and you will see a small island with the remains of houses on it on a cultivation shelf high above the sea, with nothing on either side but rock and heather. Ask yourself the question who lived here and when was it evacuated.

Altnaharra at the west end of Loch Naver

The answer could be the story of all this coast today, but for one saving grace. It opens in the clearances when people, forcibly removed from the straths to make way for sheep, had to settle on the rocky coast. In these hard times three young couples went to that island of Eilean nan Ron, built houses, fished, killed seals for blubber, broke the ground for cultivation, cut peats and founded a settlement. That was in 1820.

There was hardship, but there must have been adventure, the women working the crofts, bearing children, mending nets and spinning wool for clothing, while the men fished cod and haddock, drying it for winter storage in a special cave whose currents of air had a magic property of keeping the fish soft, so that it still tasted fresh months after it was caught.

Inshore fishing gave way to herring fishing as the population multiplied, the men chasing the shoals from Stornoway to Mallaig in early summer, switching to the East Coast, working south as far as East Anglia, not returning until November.

While the men were away the cattle were taken to the mainland hills, grazing high pastures where the young women lived in shielings, making butter, crowdie and cheese, taking it back to the island in kegs. The whole way of life was communal, the men at sea, the women on the land. When a new house was needed they blasted the rocks from an island quarry, dressed the stones, and hauled the wood and slate, lime and sand from the harbour.

The beginning of the twentieth century was the time of maximum prosperity for Eilean nan Ron with 70 on the island and 18 children on the school roll. The population ceiling had been reached, however, and no more newly-wed couples could set up house. Then came the 1914 war. Eighteen men left and seventeen returned to find the fishing ruined. Nor were they contented any more with the remoteness of island life. Family by family they withdrew to Australia, Canada, the United States or to the mainland, so that by 1938 only twelve people remained, eight of them old. Eilean nan Ron was evacuated on a stormy night in December, and the story told to the *Northern Times* by islander John George Mackay, was reprinted as a pamphlet.

I said that this depopulation story would be true of the whole coast but for one saving grace. This is

Dounreay, the atomic station which is holding together some of these coastal communities, by regular wages and a modern job within daily bus range of home. The men commute from their remote road-ends in Sutherland to Caithness five days a week, working their crofts in their spare time, or letting land to other crofters.

Willie Mackay of Invernaver with six crofts has 30 acres of arable land scattered over several miles. Not an easy way of working. In addition, he has 300 sheep on the hills; a full-time job for any man you would think, but Willie has to supplement his income by working the salmon nets on the River Naver or he would not be able to keep going.

The 30 acres of arable are required to feed 11 breeding cows, their followers and a bull. Willie has a tractor, a motor van and modern implements bought with hard work over the last twenty years but the low prices he gets for his stock never match the increasing costs of production. Yet he is unlikely to give up, for he is in love with the land, the scenery and the wildlife of Invernaver which he does not take for granted.

No wonder, for the cliffs, yellow with blown sand, have the look of perpetual sunshine, and from the ridge where he keeps his sheep his view runs from the Orkneys across Ben Loyal to Ben Hope. The country is small-scale where the rocky edge of Druim Chuibhe ends on sandhills and a 50-ft escarpment of raised beach, with stone circles, the remains of a broch, chambered cairns and burial cists of Bronze Age and Iron Age times. Just across the Naver is another broch and a virtual graveyard of tumuli. Here is the finest assemblage of boreal plant communities in northern Scotland, and in early summer the place is a hanging garden of arctic-alpine plants.

Just a mile west along the bay you come to the Borgie estuary, where the grassy outlines of the old village of Lon are discernible, dating back to the Norse settlers of the ninth century, it is thought. Indeed it is possible that the crofting system practised by the Norsemen in these Borgie and Naver valleys remained virtually unchanged until the clearances and the coming of sheep. On the coast the dispossessed people kept the old system, and that is what we see today.

'Oh yes, we're a very persistent people,' said an old crofter in one of the townships, 'but who is content with a croft nowadays? It is a job with a motor car that the younger generation want now. We have good houses, electricity, and television but these take money which you can't get by crofting. If it wasn't for Dounreay this whole coast would be as dead as Eilean nan Ron.'

The First Report of the Highlands and Islands Development Board written by Professor Sir Robert Grieve summed up the matter by saying that the croft does not and cannot, except in rare cases, support the crofter as a full-time pursuit because of its fundamental instability, but makes the point: '. . . if one had to look now for a way of life which would keep that number of people in such relatively intractable territory, it would be difficult to contrive a better system'.

By 'better system' he means a method of maintaining human communities and the road and communication services along with them. At the lowest estimate crofting maintains a living countryside which the rest of the country enjoys for recreation. Now for the quote: 'But its future depends on other employment support. This the Board accepts as a clear challenge and duty; and one important element must be by way of small industrial growth points promoted by powerful and attractive inducements. Forestry and tourism must be other aids in suitable places.'

The burning of kelp was the industry which enabled the dispossessed Highlanders to survive and multiply on a potato diet, until the bottom fell out of the market due to tariffs being removed from the import of barilla. The Highlanders tried seasonal labouring on Lowland farms but were outnumbered by an even poorer people – the unfortunate Irish. Potato blight was an added disaster. There was only one road left open, migration, and it was the one that most folk took, sailing away to a new life in Canada on overcrowded ships at a fare of £3.

They left behind a Highland problem which sheep and sporting estates could not solve, and it is still with us. Sutherland is classic ground to study how not to treat a land and its people. In the carve-up of the land which by ancient right belonged to them they were betrayed by their chiefs who sold what did not belong to them.

The historian T C Smout in his *History of the*

Scottish People 1560–1830 sums up his chapter on congestion and clearance with the words:

'In the last resort, however, it is possible that nothing could have been done that would have provided the Highlands with an alternative to congestion or clearance. The grim facts of economic geography have, time and again, defeated the good intentions of planners. It could not pay to make textiles in the north because the mills of the central belt, and of Lancashire and Yorkshire were so much better located for the market. It was hard to make substantial investments in fishing pay for the same reason. The marketing of cattle, and even of wool itself, was hampered by bad transport when competition sharpened. An area so high, so wet and so remote is at a perpetual disadvantage in a modern economy, and no amount of wishful thinking can make it otherwise. There were men in the eighteenth century who expected to build cities the size of Liverpool in the Western Highlands: there have been men ever since with one version or another of this dream. But perhaps it is all to the good that they do not allow themselves to be diverted from their vision by the study of so dismaying a subject as history.'

It has been argued that the Estate Factors to the Countess of Sutherland were trying to better the lot of the people when in 1811 they gave this statement quoted by Smout in his book:

'Sheep farms are paying well on the Sutherland estates. The number of Chieviots are now about 15,000. More ground will be laid off for the same mode of husbandry, without decreasing the population. Situations in various ways will be fixed on for the people. Fishing stations, in which mechanics will be settled; inland villages, with carding machines; moors and detached spots calculated for the purpose will be found, but the people must work. The industrious will be encouraged and protected, but the slothful must remove or starve, as man was not born to be idle, but to gain his bread by the sweat of his brow.'

Look at the date of that statement, and remember that the peak of the Sutherland evictions was 1814 and 1819, when houses and furniture went up in smoke and even a cat was thrown back into the blaze. The money the Countess did spend on improvements was bitter fuel to the flame of Strathnaver.

The people submitted when they should have fought, but the best of the men who might have led them had got out a long time before, seeing no future for themselves.

Lochs of the Brora Basin
Loch Brora

Loch Brora lies just three miles upstream from the salmon river which passes under the town bridge to the North Sea, and the way to it from there leads past the only colliery in the Far North so a pause should be made to take account of the whitewashed buildings, the little chimney and the winding gear of what is an important industrial monument, for this is the oldest colliery in Scotland. The oldest colliery, but it produces the youngest coal, Jurrasic as distinct from the more normal Carboniferous deposits, the Brora coal being a mere 125 million years old compared to 260 million years of the older seams.

Records here go back to 1529 when out-crop coal was used to make salt from sea water. The circular stone-lined shaft sunk around 1810 was a hundred years ahead of its time in technique, and was to be copied by the mining world using concrete instead of rectangular wooden shafts. The pit, threatened with closure when the National Coal Board refused to nationalise it, is thriving again under co-operative ownership by the miners themselves.

So before going to the loch, look at the colliery with more than passing interest, for it is one that has never known a labour dispute. Reflect too that this is the only place in Britain where miners are also crofters, some of them having quite substantial holdings on the green hills above the river. They earn high wages, and they have won a silver cup for high productivity of coal in recent times. The discovery of a new rich seam will assure the future of the colliery for a few generations to come.

Loch Brora seen from the top of the bold Carrol Rock is constricted into three nearly separate blobs, the biggest to the north. These narrows are caused by the build-up of alluvium from the entering streams, the total length being $3\frac{1}{2}$ miles, with a maximum breadth of nearly $\frac{1}{2}$ a mile near the head, though the mean is only $\frac{1}{4}$ of a mile. The maximum depth of 66 ft is in the middle; the mean is $22\frac{1}{2}$ ft.

The Bathymetric Survey records four basins in order from the outlet as follows:

1 A shallow basin with a maximum depth of 31 ft shallowing to 7 ft.

2　The basin which contains Eilean nam Faoileag, an island once fortified, and used in a later period by the Earl of Sutherland as a hunting lodge. The maximum depth is 43 ft shallowing to 9 ft.

3　The third and deepest basin containing the maximum depth of 66 ft shallowing to 4 and 7 ft.

4　In the fourth the depth is 59 ft to the south-east and 64 ft to the north-east.

The fishing for salmon, sea trout and brown trout is good, May and June being the best months. Burghfield House Hotel and the Sutherland Arms Hotel have fishing rights, £1 per day and £1 per boat.

From the wooded loch a little excursion can be made by a path up the Blackwater to a Pictish broch known as Castle Cole on a narrow neck above the river in a fine defence situation of crag and defile. There are remains of fortifications also on Craig Bar on the south side of Loch Brora and numerous tumuli in the neighbourhood, green hummocks without history.

Of the walled fortifications on Eilean nam Faoileag there is one traditional story told; of an invasion of Caithness men which caused the locals to flee behind the defences of the island. Unable to get at them, the enemy then began damming the outlet of the loch in the hope of flooding them out, which would be a slow process to say the least.

The islanders were alarmed however, and in the darkness of the night took to their boats and were being pursued on land when they met with members of the clan Gunn coming to their assistance. A battle was fought and the Caithness men were given their due. The narrows where the enemy tried to build their dam is still known as Daman, or Davan, meaning of course a dam.

Lochs of the Helmsdale Basin

Lochs an Ruathair, Coire nan Meann, Leum a' Chlamhain,
Araich-Lin, Truid air Sgithiche, nan Cuinne, a'Chlair,
Baddanloch, Allt an Fheàrna and na Moine

These moorland sheets of water lie in the rather
featureless country between Strath Ullie, noted for its
gold, and Strath Halladale which drops enchantingly
to Melvich Bay on the north coast; and in springtime
if you motor this single-track road you have to watch
out for lambs for the place is jumping with them.
Rail and road run together to Forsinard, where the
line swings away east to Caithness over roadless peat-
hags. Immediately south of Forsinard and half way to
Kinbrace lies Loch an Ruathair.

This is the loch nearest to the source of the Helmsdale and it contains trout and char in its rather
shallow oval of water. Length 1½ miles, breadth ¾ mile
and maximum depth 26 ft with a mean of half that
amount, the bottom is flattish, its overspill joining the
Helmsdale below Kinbrace.

Loch Coire nan Meann. Famed for its good trout,
this shallow loch which also contains char, is most
easily reached from the branch road which goes
west into Strathnaver. Roughly circular in shape
with a diameter of ½ a mile it drains by a short stream
into the next loch to be mentioned. It is a simple basin
with a maximum depth of 33 ft and a mean of 11½ ft.

Loch Leum a' Chlamhain. Only ¼ of a mile
separates this loch from the above, and it too is good
for large trout. The length is 1⅔ miles with a maximum
breadth of just over ½ a mile, and the bottom is in two
basins covered by shallower water between. The
maximum depth of south and north basins is nearly
the same, 51 ft and 50 ft respectively, the mean for
the whole loch being 19½ ft.

Loch Araich-Lin or Arichlinie is a tiny loch
immediately north-west of Kinbrace and contains
trout and char in its shallow waters whose maximum
depth is only 7 ft with a mean of 4½ ft. The length is
¾ of a mile and the breadth ⅓ of a mile. Inflowing
streams are gradually silting the loch with alluvium.

Truid air Sgithiche, or Truderscaig, is another fine
trout loch, and presumably private like all the rest.
Lying due east of Ben Kliberick, the outline is triangular with the apex pointing north-east out of
which the burn flows to Loch nan Cuinne. The length

is just under a mile with a maximum width of $\frac{2}{3}$ of a mile and a maximum depth of 12 ft. Shallow and flat-bottomed, the mean depth is 6 ft.

Loch nan Cuinne. Known locally as Rimsdale Loch. Garvault Hotel, Kinbrace have brown trout fishing rights, and must include Lochs a' Chlair and Baddan-loch for these waters are virtually continuous, though 100 yards of stream separates the first from the other two.

Loch nan Cuinne is 3 miles long and of variable width, the mean being just over $\frac{2}{3}$ of a mile, though the central portion is $\frac{3}{4}$ of a mile broad. The maximum depth is 28 ft in the widest part, with an overall mean of $12\frac{1}{2}$ ft.

Loch a' Chlair. The passage between the first loch and this one is 5 ft deep and there is a great feeling of space, given presence by the distant peaks of Hope, Loyal, Morven and nearby Kliberick and Armine. This irregular water which is continuous with the next is measured separately. The length east to west is just over $1\frac{1}{2}$ miles with a north to south width of $1\frac{1}{3}$ miles, the mean being $\frac{3}{4}$ of a mile. The maximum depth is 32 ft with a mean of $13\frac{1}{2}$ ft.

The Helmsdale river, looking to Strath Ullie

Loch Baddanloch. This appendage is 1¾ miles long and 1 mile in maximum width, with a maximum depth of 42 ft and a mean of 17 ft. The level of these lochs can rise fairly quickly.

Loch Allt an Fheàrna. This mile-long loch of pear shape is ½ a mile in maximum width and is 36 ft at deepest with a mean of 14 ft. It lies close to the above named into which it flows by a short stream.

Loch na Moine. The Helmsdale River emerges from this loch which is only 2½ miles from Kinbrace. Only 8 ft in maximum depth, with a mean of 4½ ft, it contains salmon and trout in its 1 mile long by ¾ of a mile wide waters. Its smallness is remarkable considering that it receives drainage from an area 400 times greater than its size. One of the delights of this neighbourhood is the preponderance of greenshank in the wild floes, their sharp echoing cries a perfect complement to the wailing pipes of golden plover. On smaller lochs which must go unmentioned I have found the common scoter breeding, and there may be the odd wood sandpiper nesting if you know where to look.

The scene of the first goldrush was the Kildonan Burn after a round piece of gold weighing over half an ounce was found in the gravelly bed. The Duke of Sutherland had a ring made from it, but although a great deal of searching was done, nothing more was found for half a century until a native prospector Robert Gilchrist returned from Australia. He found gold near Kildonan Farm, alerted other prospectors who soon made a strike in the Suisgill Burn just to the north. Strikes were soon being made in other burns at Kinbrace and Berridale.

The goldrush settlements of tents was called Baile-an-Oir, 'City of Gold', and a signpost marks the spot today. The cost of staking a 40-square-foot claim in 1869 was £1 sterling per month. Regulations stipulated that one tenth of any gold found had to go to the Crown, and excisemen were on hand to extract their due.

The Bank of England analysed a sample and valued it at 759·9 gold, 22·7 silver, with alloy present at 17·4, including copper. Well-equipped miners were getting enough to give them 50p a day, though casual 'panners' were not so successful. But the 500 miners produced a local trade boom in Helmsdale and even the great Duke was pleased enough to send an ox and

a cask of beer from Dunrobin Castle. He even organised a dinner for 300 miners at which the man who had sparked off the strike carved the joint.

The big goldrush did not survive the winter. It might have done if the miners had been permitted to explore towards the loch systems described in this chapter, but the sheep farmers and the sportsmen and gamekeepers wanted rid of the miners and were glad to see them go down the valley. The Excise figure of the gold taken was put around £11,000, but it would be a poor Highlander who would declare everything to the Crown. No doubt a few fortunes were made, and they may be made again by modern exploration companies who are showing renewed interest.

Meantime the richest local mineral is the Brora coal just over the hills.

The Kildonan Burn, scene of a goldstrike (left)

A great skua (below)

Caithness–Lochs of the Wick Basin
Lochs Scarmclate, Watten and Hempriggs

Ask nine out of ten people where the most northerly point of the British mainland lies and they will tell you John o' Groats. They would be wrong, for the true north point is Dunnet Head. South and west of it lie the low level lochs of the county which the Norseman named Caithness when they colonised it about A.D. 880. The local tribes displaced fought like wildcats, and are remembered by the word Caithness which is derived from Catti. The boundary between Sutherland and Caithness follows closely the geological division of the old red stone where the peaks come to an end in Morvern and moorlands.

But it is by no means as dreary as Volume XV of the new *Statistical Account of Scotland* makes out, which reads:

'The general appearance of the county is flat and uninteresting; the only hills of any eminence forming the boundary with Sutherland. A great proportion of the ground consists of flat moor and heath, and there being no extent of trees, the interior has a dreary appearance. Along the sea coast, which is generally

Caithness – a country of moors and shallow lochs

bold and rocky, the appearance improves; and, from the improvements now going on in various quarters, a more cheerful and pleasant aspect is given to it, especially along the high road from the south towards Thurso. There are a few sheets of water, but none of any extent or peculiar beauty of appearance, and there are no navigable rivers.'

Travel there and you come across Norse names like Tister, Stemster, Wester and Hoy. There is even a 'Greenland', and no false description either to mislead any innocent to become a colonist, for it is a truly fertile place of swaying grasses loud with the trilling of skylarks, a farming rather than a crofting country, with broad fields full of sheep and cattle until you come to Brough, where the feeling is of being suddenly transported to the Hebrides, with dozens of white houses dotting the green strips and large peat stacks by every door. The blue sea and the rocky headland beyond the sweep of Dunnet Bay add to the feeling.

And like the Outer Hebrides, there is sharp contrast when suddenly the crofting land peters out and you are in a world of peaty hills and bog cotton lochs – except that this little world ends in a plunge of over 340 feet of cliff, and perched on the very brink is the dazzling pencil-stalk of Dunnet Head lighthouse.

Sit on that cliff-top and you look down on rows of guillemots and razorbills packing the ledges like penguins, with far below them thousands upon thousands of snow-white kittiwakes milling round their swallow-nests, hung dizzily on the most vertical places. Puffins, with red legs hung out like rudders, scurry back and forth continually to their burrows on the earthy parts of the cliff.

It was near here I found the only pair of great skuas then breeding on the mainland of Scotland, like huge brown gulls by a little loch where a red-throated diver sat on two eggs. And not so far away there were black-tailed godwits breeding, while on a crag only 700 feet above sea-level a golden eagle was feeding two well grown chicks. From the eyrie I could look past the big egg of the Dounreay Atomic Station to the Orkneys while listening to the reeling notes of dunlin and the thin pipings of golden plover. It's no wonder that the men who come to work in Dounreay grow to love Caithness.

Certainly the best of this north-east tip of Scotland

is the sea coast from the sands of Reay on to Duncansby Head east of John o' Groats where that delightful primula the Scottish primrose brightens the turf with its purplish flowers, each with a yellow eye. It is found nowhere else but on this north coast from Sutherland to the Orkneys, so it is worth more than a passing glance. It is believed to have evolved from *Primula farinosa*, developing smaller and fewer flowers after the Ice Age and becoming self-pollinating.

The wild seas have been known to hurl stones up the cliffs and break the windows of Dunnet Head Lighthouse. English trawlermen call the Pentland Firth Hell's Gate whose flood-tide current runs at ten miles an hour west to east at new and full moon. Then comes the reverse flow and a mighty churning up process takes place as the currents fight it out making the water rage on the calmest day and producing ferocious seas when wind and tide are against each other. I have rounded the Caithness coast in a trawler bound for Aberdeen and can speak from personal experience of the dangerous passage.

What of the lochs? Loch Scarmclate is a typical shallow Caithness loch in boulder clay whose maximum depth is only 5 ft. Triangular in shape with a maximum length of nearly a mile, the maximum breadth is just over $\frac{1}{2}$ a mile. Situated in farming land, its floor used to be dredged for a white and calcareous mud found to the south of the island. Spread on the fields it marled the land.

Loch Watten. This 3-mile-long loch has a larger superficial area than any other Caithness loch. Situated mid-way between Wick and Thurso the maximum breadth is $\frac{3}{4}$ of a mile and the maximum depth is 12 ft, though half of it is less than 6 ft deep. Salmon, sea trout and brown trout fishing are available from 75p a day, details appended below.

Loch Hempriggs. Situated 2 miles south-west of Wick this sub-circular loch has a maximum depth of 8 ft and a diameter of $\frac{3}{4}$ of a mile.

For fishing Loch Watten apply:
Lochview Farmhouse, Watten. Telephone Watten 663
Portland Arms Hotel, Lybster. Telephone Lybster 208.

Lochs Wester, Heilen and St John's
Loch of Wester is a mile long and is so close to sea-level

at Sinclair's Bay that high tides find their way into the freshwater and make it salt for a time. Only 3 ft deep and shallower than the short river connecting it to the sea, it contains salmon, brown trout and sea trout. Permits are available from Lochview Farmhouse, Watten and Mr Charles Dunnet, Aukhorn, Lyth. Charges from 75p per day.

Loch Heilen. Two miles east of Dunnet Bay, this $1\frac{1}{2}$-mile-long by $\frac{1}{2}$-mile broad loch has a maximum depth of 5 ft and contains brown trout. Permits from Mr Pottinger, Loch End Farm, Barrock, also Loch Watten Farmhouse.

St John's Loch. This small sub-circular loch has a mean depth of only $4\frac{1}{2}$ ft and a maximum of 7 ft in its less than $\frac{1}{2}$ a mile diameter. Fishing is £1 per day with boat from Northern Sands Hotel, Dunnet. Castle Mey, residence of the Queen Mother lies east along the coast.

Lochs of the Thurso Basin

Loch More is another sub-circular loch less than $\frac{1}{2}$ a mile in diameter with a maximum depth of 7 ft, half of the flat bottom being covered by less than 5 ft of water. Thirteen miles south of Thurso it has a big reputation for salmon and trout fishing which is private.

Lochs of the Forss Basin

Loch Shurrey. This $1\frac{1}{4}$-mile-long loch lies 7 miles south of Reay in moorland country. Width less than $\frac{1}{2}$ a mile, the maximum depth is 7 ft with a mean of 4 ft.

Loch Calder is the deepest loch in Caithness, and it was on its shore that Earl Rognvald Kali, founder of St Magnus Cathedral and ruler of Orkney and Shetland, was struck on the face and killed. That incident occurred on 20 August 1158 at a place called Forsie, but his relics and the mutilated skull were not found until the last century in a cavity high in the north pillar of the Cathedral choir. This great find in the cathedral was to be rivalled in 1919 during restoration work when it was noticed that some stones high in the south pillar of the choir needed attention. They revealed a cavity containing bones and the battered skull of Earl Magnus who 804 years before, almost to the day, had been executed in a manner of his choice, by being struck on the middle of the head.

The skull in the box showed the axe wound to be as described in the Orkneyinga Saga thus confirming the account of the execution which took place on Egilsay in 1115.

Think of the good Earls then, who were canonised to Sainthood, when you go to this loch which is a true rock basin in Caithness flagstones with a bottom of 85 ft. The length is 2¼ miles with a breadth of nearly 1 mile. The fishing is for brown trout, and permits are available from Lochview Farmhouse, Watten, or from 'The Tackle Shop', 23 Sinclair Street, Thurso.

There are plenty of other good fishing lochs in Caithness, mostly small and all of them shallow in a variety of settings where the main feature is the vast horizon and open skies. Water permits and further information can be obtained by writing to the County Development Officer, Wick, or to Thurso Fisheries Ltd, Thurso East, Thurso.

Account too should be taken of the numerous brochs of Caithness, sited near some of the lochs and at places where landings could be made from the sea as at Dounreay, Lybster, Scrabster, Castletown, Ham, Kirk o' Tongue, Borrogie, Skirsa Head, Freswickn Nybster, Tong Head, Keiss, Ackergill, Staxigoe, Papigoe, Hempriggs, Ulbster, Bruan, Occumster, Latheron etc.

The brochs are one of the mysteries of Scotland, for they occur nowhere else in the world and a great weight of literature has grown up round them. Theories as to the origins of these towers which rose as high as 60 feet will be discussed in another chapter. Whoever built them in Caithness took full advantage of the Caithness flagstones which are so easily worked here that they do service as fences in some fields. The Old Red Sandstone of which the flags are composed is rich in fossil fish forms, and the total thickness of the series is estimated at 14,500 feet.

The numerous chambered cairns in Caithness are of two types, long horned cairns and round cairns with the same features of those in Argyll. It is thought that the builders of these ancient burial cairns came from the south-west. Norse burial finds in the cairns reveal connections with the regions of Møre, Rogaland and Trondelag in West Norway, dating from the ninth century.

Sir John Sinclair, born in Thurso Castle in 1745,

also left his monument in the twenty-one volumes of *The Statistical Account of Scotland* describing every parish in Scotland. Completed in 1799 it is an invaluable source book for the times. An initiator of agricultural reforms, it is to be regretted that his best suggestion was never taken up, namely that the land-lords should combine with Highland tenants and run sheep farms as co-operative enterprises. The land-owners, greedy for rent, preferred a different solution which led to the inhuman clearances.

Orkney and its Lochs

Lochs Stenness, Harray, Bosquoy, Sabiston, Isbister,
Kirkbister, Tankerness, Swannay, Boardhouse, Hundland,
Skaill, Muckle Water, Peerie and Hoglins

A sail of only 28 miles from Scrabster in Caithness
takes you to Stromness in Orkney passing the Old
Man of Hoy on the way. Step along the flagstoned
street where the gable-ends point to the sea and
narrow lanes lead steeply down to little harbours and
you have the feeling of being abroad, a feeling
emphasised if someone asks you if you come from
Scotland. Orkney, which was Scandinavian until the
fifteenth century, still regards herself as being different.
And so it is.

Man exploring from the Mediterranean was quick
to discover the advantages of the Orkneys, as the
Stone Age village of Skara Brae on the Bay of Skail
testifies. Within a very short distance of Stromness the
various stages of man's culture can be traced for 4,000
years through megalithic tombs and stone circles to
the chapels of early Christians. The Norsemen left us
a wonderful literature in the Orkneyinga Saga. They
built St Magnus Cathedral in Kirkwall, in sound of
whose bells live one fifth of the 19,000 or so people
who inhabit the islands today.

The small population relative to the amount of good
land explains some of the prosperity of modern
Orkney, which is a countryside of small farms, not
crofts. Sixty years ago when the population was 30,000
the average land holding was $16\frac{1}{2}$ acres. Today it is
35 acres, which in Orkney means good soil made of
red sandstone, which is porous and retains heat. This
is no peaty acid soil as in the Outer Hebrides, where
the hard gneiss allows no proper drainage. Also the
rainfall in Orkney is only 35 in. a year compared to
60 in. in Lewis. In Orkney 35 acres can support 35 or
more Jersey or Ayrshire cows without being over-
stocked.

The milk goes to Kirkwall Creamery, a favourite
retreat of holiday visitors on wet days. This is where
the Claymore butter and Orkney cheese are made,
and skim milk is converted into powder by modern
machinery. Output has risen over 20 times since 1946.
The local distillery has the biggest pot-still in
Scotland. Straw-backed Orkney chairs are still being
hand-made by the local coffin maker.

Hoy today is the saddest island, almost empty now that Lyness is no longer a naval base. The social and operational centre of 20,000 servicemen is now a ghost town littered with concrete debris and other sad remains. The health of the various communities scattered between the North Isles and the South Isles of Orkney is better, centring on the land and sea, not on the whims of the navy or industry. On these green islands there are 3,000 good farms owning between them the biggest number of tractors and motor cars to be found anywhere in Europe – proportionate to population. Their people are workers, so energetic that they find time to gather seaweed and export it to South Uist in spare hours of their days. From these islands sailed the home fleet in war. Stromness was once the northern port of call for rice ships, and here the Hudson Bay whaling fleet used to take on water and men. Nowadays planes from the Continent call to buy Orkney lobsters and the Fishermen's Society have thoughts of turning land-locked Scapa Flow into a gigantic lobster farm. There is always a stir in Stromness or Kirkwall because they exist to serve the islands, shuttling forth the imports and exports which keep Orkney alive. The pace of life is fast on Mainland where the creamery is a factory clock gearing everyone to its time for collecting the milk and handling it. On the smaller islands such as Westray there is no clock, the emphasis is on beef cattle and poultry, so nobody appears to be in a hurry, but they have an inter-island plane service which is a great asset.

How did their forbears live? Take the case of Svein Asleifsson, a viking who lived like an Earl in the Orkneys and died in Dublin fighting in the year 1171. This is how the Orkneyinga Saga describes his life: 'It was Svein's custom to spend the winter at home in Gairsay, where he always kept 80 men at his own expense. He had the largest drinking hall in the whole of Orkney. Svein was always busy in spring, when he would have great quantities of seed sown, doing much of the work himself. When the sowing was done, he would go off every spring on a raiding expedition to harry the coasts of the Hebrides and Ireland, returning home after midsummer: and this he called his spring raiding. Then he would stay at home until the crops were cut and the grain harvested. Then he

overleaf: Stromness, Orkney

An alley in Stromness leads to the sea

would go on another expedition, and did not return home until a month after the beginning of winter; and this he called his autumn raiding.'

When an Orkney man talks about Mainland he does not mean the country across the Pentland Firth but the biggest of the seventy islands which scatter over a large area of sea. Only Mainland in the group has changed its shape of recent times by acquiring a tail in the shape of Burray and South Ronaldshay which are linked by causeways known as the Churchill Barriers. A road runs over the top, and as you drive along the top reflect that this was where the Royal Oak was sunk by a U-boat with a loss of 800 lives early in the war, while on land the first British civilian was killed by air attack.

It is on Mainland which comprises about 200 sq. miles and has over 200 miles of good motoring roads that we find the important lochs, all of them good for fishing and all of them free, hence the description of Orkney as 'This Angling Paradise'. Even the salmon

Inside the Norse cathedral of St Magnus in Kirkwall

here are free, for they are mostly taken in salt water
or at burn-mouths by rod and line using lob worms.
The locals go for them in September and do well, even
if the fish are advanced in spawn.

Where the burns enter the sea is also good for sea
trout on their way to spawn. The worm is the favourite
local bait and average fish are from $1\frac{1}{2}$ to 2 lbs though
fish three times that size are frequently taken. Now
for the lochs, which are so good for sea trout and brown
trout and of such high general interest.

Loch of Stenness and Loch of Harray are separated
from each other only by a narrow neck of land on
which with a fine sense of the dramatic early man
built one of the most exciting monuments in Britain,
the Ring of Brognar, a gaunt Stonehenge giving
brooding character to the great expanse of water and
low land under the great changing skies, Harray to
the east and Stenness to the west with a sea passage
only a short distance southward.

Loch of Stenness is in fact salt, and its salinity

Orkney: the most agricultural of the islands of Scotland

affects Loch Harray, though this has been controlled to a great extent by the Orkney Angling Association fitting flaps at the Bridge of Brogar outflow to reduce the sea water entering. The tide which does the damage enters from the Bay of Ireland under Bridge of Waith, and it seems to suit the brown trout for the largest on record from Orkney was taken from the Loch of Stenness, weight 29½ lbs, and its cast is in Stromness Museum.

Length 4 miles and breadth 1½ miles in the bulging centre, the water is fresh only at the surface, the maximum depth of 17 ft occurring at the south-eastern extremity, while the mean is 10½ ft. On the shore just north of where the sea plunges in at Bridge of Waith is Unston Cairn, one of the most famous of the Orkney burial cairns because of the pottery found here unburnt and burnt, with human and animal bones.

The pottery, found in 1884, has been estimated to date from at least 1500 B.C. and is akin to that dis-

Gathering seaweed at Finstown for export to South Uist

covered in the lowest stratum of Windmill Hill in Wiltshire. This largest collection of Neolithic pottery ever found at one site in Scotland is enshrined in the term 'Unston Ware' to indicate this special type of ornate vase. Barley marks on the shards show that grain must have been cultivated in the Stone Age. No doubt the vases originally contained food to see the dead on their last journey.

Loch of Harray. This wide water, $4\frac{2}{3}$ miles by $1\frac{3}{4}$ miles, is the largest and most renowned of the Orkney fishing lochs. Situated in a lowland mixture of moorland, wet meadows and farmland, it is a shallow rock basin in Middle Old Red Flagstones, maximum depth 14 ft and mean 9 ft. The feeding must be good, for the growth rate of fish is said to be ahead of all the other lochs. May and June are the best months for brown trout, the average being around 1 lb. Wading in the rocky islets of the west shore is not difficult, but a ghillie is recommended for boating because of the rocky shore. Apart from Merkister Hotel, the local farmers have boats for hire.

Just a step from the southern tip of Loch Harray lies the sun-hat shape of the grassy knoll known as Maes Howe, 24 ft high and 115 ft in diameter with a tunnel leading into the heart of the finest Megalithic burial cairn in the British Isles. A stone tomb of superb construction, with cells opening off the main chamber; its interest is heightened by the fact that it contains the runic scribblings of the Norsemen who raided it, the greatest number of these scrawls to be found anywhere in the world.

One of them reads: 'These runes were incised by the best runester in the west, using the axe that Gauk Trandilsson once owned in the south of Iceland.'

Another reads: 'The Jerusalem pilgrims broke in here.'

Still another: 'Ingigerd is the sweetest woman there is.'

As well as the branch-like strokes of the runic writing there are drawings of a lion, a walrus, and a serpent-knot, a unique historical record which makes mention of treasures removed from the tomb and gives bits of information which tie up with the Sagas. The craftsmanship of the building is said to be unsurpassed in Western Europe.

Loch of Bosquoy. Situated near the north-east tip of Loch Harray in boggy meadow this small shallow loch is fishable when the weather is too stormy for the bigger waters. Length $\frac{2}{3}$ of a mile by $\frac{1}{3}$ of a mile, the depth is 5 ft maximum with a mean of $2\frac{1}{2}$ ft. Weeds in mid-summer make fishing difficult. The fish average half a pound or less.

Loch of Sabiston. Lies $1\frac{1}{2}$ miles north of Loch Harray on a boggy flat under the Hill of Greenay, length $\frac{1}{2}$ a mile, breadth $\frac{1}{4}$ of a mile, maximum depth 3 ft. Keep an eye open for hen harriers and short-eared owls wavering over the moor. Their main prey is the Orkney vole and both are ground nesters. The elegant hen harrier, flickering on long wings, may take a vicious swipe at you if you get too close to its young and may strike and draw blood, the right kind of action to deter the trespasser, I would say.

Loch of Isbister. Situated near the village of Twatt in boggy ground this small loch is $\frac{2}{3}$ of a mile long by nearly $\frac{2}{3}$ of a mile broad, the maximum depth being 3 ft and the mean $1\frac{1}{2}$ ft. Trout of 1 lb and over are taken here in May and June.

Loch of Kirkbister. This loch, 5 miles south-west of Kirkwall, is in the Parish of Orphir and is recommended for beginners in fishing, for the stock of small trout is so great that failure to bring home something is almost impossible. Length 1¾ miles by ½ a mile broad, the maximum depth is 6 ft and the mean 4 ft. Any visit here should take account of the round church of Orphir, a remaining fragment of a twelfth century church built to the model of the Church of the Holy Sepulchre in Jerusalem. It is attributed to Earl Hakon who put to death Earl Magnus.

The well in Stromness

THERE WATERED HERE
THE HUDSON BAY COY'S SHIPS
1670 - 1891

CAPT. COOK'S VESSELS
RESOLUTION AND DISCOVERY
1780

SIR JOHN FRANKLIN'S SHIPS
EREBUS AND TERROR
ON ARCTIC EXPLORATION
1845

ALSO THE MERCHANT VESSELS
OF FORMER DAYS

WELL SEALED UP 1931

The ring of Brognar between Lochs Harray and Stenness

Unston, the most famous of Orkney burial cairns

Fishing the Loch of Stenness

Maeshone, a fine example of a megalithic burial cairn

Here is a passage from the Orkneyinga Saga, amply supported by evidence on the ground:
'At Orphir there was a large drinking-hall, with a door in the south side-wall right at the eastern gable; facing this door was a magnificent church, and some steps led down from the hall to the church.'

Look beyond the semi-circular apse of the sanctuary and you can trace the stone foundations of that hall, together with an opening at the eastern end where steps led down to the church, the place where that 'Ultimate Viking' Svein Asleifsson committed murder after rowing across the Pentland Firth in his galley on Christmas Eve. The ruins and the runes as at Maes Howe, here and elsewhere, square with the Sagas whose authenticity is beyond doubt. No ancient history in stone has been invested with so much life, thanks to the Icelandic storytellers.

Loch of Tankerness lies east of Kirkwall across Inganess Bay on a peninsula. Roughly triangular in shape this mile-long loch by $\frac{1}{2}$ a mile has a maximum depth of 7 ft and a mean of $4\frac{1}{2}$ ft.

Loch of Swannay. This large elliptical loch is the most northerly on Mainland and is popular for fishing competitions. One angler has taken out 42 brown trout in a day weighing 69 lb 10 oz. Boats are readily available and the west shore is recommended as safest for wading. The length is 2 miles with maximum breadth of $\frac{2}{3}$ of a mile and the maximum depth is 16 ft with a mean of 9 ft. Shallows and rocks occur at various points, so fishermen using outboard motors on their boats have to be careful. The main road round the island skirts the top of the loch so access is easy.

Loch of Boardhouse is at the north-west tip of Mainland half a mile east of Birsay. The Orkney Angling Association have a boat house here on the west shore and an evening competition is held on this good fishing loch every May. The length is 2 miles, the maximum breadth is $\frac{2}{3}$ of a mile, the maximum depth is 9 ft and the mean 6 ft. Boats are available from the Barony Hotel and from various local people in Birsay.

Loch of Hundland. This triangular loch lies between the last two described and like the other two tends to be weedy after June. The length is $1\frac{1}{3}$ miles and the breadth just over $\frac{1}{2}$ a mile, with a maximum depth of 7 ft and a mean of 4 ft. It is partly in flagstones and partly in boulder clay.

Travellers in this area should pay a visit to the tidal
island of Birsay, accessible except between three
hours before and after high tide. It should be noted
however that high water here is one hour before high
water at Kirkwall. On this island the mightiest Earl
to rule Orkney built his palace, having demolished all
opposition, to rule with benevolence the Northern
Isles, the Western Isles and much of Scotland and
Ireland. That ruler of most ugly countenance was
Earl Thorfinn, whose empire fragmented with his
death in the eleventh century. It was from this tidal
island he ruled, though the sea has eaten away most
of the palace on the edge of the cliff.

His body lies within the ruins of the Romanesque
church dedicated to St Peter. Earl Thorfinn had been
to Rome with Macbeth, King of the Scots. He had
apparently learned a thing or two on his pilgrimage,
for there is evidence that he had central heating in his
palace and Turkish baths using the local flagstones to
give off steam from hot water thrown on them. Cross
over to Birsay then if you would see where Thorfinn
the Great lived in style, with his court.

That other Earl's palace on the Mainland at
Birsay, like Earl Patrick's palace in Kirkwall, is a
reminder of oppressive rule from Scotland which
followed the infinitely more generous days of the
Norse Earls.

Loch of Skaill. A small loch due north of Stromness
near the Bay of Skaill, one of the most interesting
places in Orkney. Triangular-shaped and containing
an artificial island of flat stones, the length of the loch
is nearly 1 mile by $\frac{1}{2}$ a mile broad, the maximum
depth being 4 ft and the mean 2 ft. Muddy bottomed
and reedy, the outflow used to power a corn mill. The
real interest about here is Skara Brae on the Bay of
Skaill beyond the boggy flats.

This Stone Age village is the finest example of its
kind and shows us the kind of furniture our forbears
used, and the way they built their huts, linking them
by passages. The settlement is in a remarkable state
of preservation, thanks to the sand that buried the
ruins until they were revealed after a great storm last
century.

Dated by fragments of pottery found, these huts
must go back to 1500 B.C. at least, yet only the roofs
have caved in, the rectangular rooms with the

The round church of Orphir

Skara Brae, a Stone Age village

Stone Age furniture, Skara Brae

Rousay, with the interior of broch in foreground

An Orcadian water-mill of horizontal type at Dounby

The horizontal water-wheel at Dounby

rounded corners, the hearths and the drains remain to indicate to us how a people who tended cows and sheep lived.

Muckle Water, Rousay. Just north-east of Mainland lies Rousay, another island rich in archaeological monuments. This narrow loch, 1 mile long by $\frac{3}{4}$ of a mile broad has a maximum depth of 20 ft and a mean of 11 ft and lies 322 ft above sea level just north of the Peerie Water.

Peerie Water. Muckle means large, and Peerie means small, the loch in question being no more than $\frac{1}{2}$ a mile long by $\frac{1}{6}$ of a mile broad. The maximum depth is 10 ft and the mean 6 ft.

Hoglins Water, Isle of Hoy. This tiny rock basin has the distinction of being the deepest loch in the Orkneys at 57 ft maximum, with a mean of 26 ft. The length is only $\frac{1}{3}$ of a mile and the breadth $\frac{1}{5}$ of a mile. The greater height of the hills of Hoy and the resultant down-cutting of ice in glacial times no doubt account for the great depth of the Hoglins basin in the Upper Old Red Sandstone, excavated when the Scottish ice flowing north-westwards over-rode the Orkneys from Caithness.

Facing out to the Pentland Firth, the great crags of Hoy are now attracting the finest rock climbers in the country. The Old Man of Hoy, that finger of rock rising 400 ft from the sea, was climbed in the sixties as a television spectacular and now it is a popular route. Then the 1,200-ft challenge of St John's Head North Wall was accepted, giving two crack climbers, Edwin Drummond and Oliver Hill 'the most difficult climb ever attempted in Britain'. They succeeded after nearly a week hanging on the face, and they called their climb 'The Longhope Route', after the men of that village in Hoy who went out on a lifeboat mission and who never came back.

Today there is a new lifeboat in Hoy and another crew ready to take to the sea when called upon.

Lochs of Shetland

Lochs Cliff, Snarravoe, Stourhoull, Watlee, Spiggie,
Clickhimin, Girlsta, Tingwall, Asta, Strom, Roer Water,
Papil Water, Winyadepla, Funzie

If you want to fish or bird-watch around the most
northerly loch in Britain then you must go to Loch
Cliff of Unst in Shetland which is considerably nearer
to Bergen in Norway than to Aberdeen in Scotland.
Ponded by gravel where the Burra Firth indents the
last land in Scotland, there is little more beyond this
loch except Hermaness and the stacks of Muckle
Flugga where the Atlantic and the North Sea fight it
out round the great gannet cliffs. Of the hundred
Shetland islands extending seventy miles, none
produces such an overwhelming feeling of timeless
austerity as Unst which in some mysterious way
reminded a friend of mine of East Africa–nor was he
thinking of darkness, rather of the vastness.

The land and seascapes of Shetland are less friendly
than the green fertility of the Orkneys, with rugged-
ness everywhere more pronounced, in cliffs and
heather, the whole cut up by innumerable fjords
called voes. Here in summer the sun is below the
horizon for only five hours in mid-June, and above it
for only five hours in mid-December. More fertile
than the Faroes, they have a similar predominance
of gales and fogs, and like them it is fishing rather
than agriculture which holds the population.

The Norse accent is unmistakable. When the
Shetlander greets you with 'Due is wylkomm', it is
almost the Norwegian 'De er velkommen'. Shetland
tongue is a mixture of the old Norn language plus
Scots, English, German and Dutch. The Faroese
people have no difficulty in understanding it since
they share the common inheritance.

There was a little corner of Shetland which was
still Norwegian in 1940 when the National Flag flew
from the mast of Lerwick Tower to show that one
Norse garrison was still out of enemy hands. It was
from these islands that the Viking invasion went into
reverse when 'The Shetland Bus' began shuttling
between Scalloway and the Norwegian coast, to take
men out and bring men in under the noses of the
enemy, just part of the war of nerves which pinned
down the occupying army and destroyed its morale.
The story has been well told by David Howarth in

The Shetland Bus.

The story of the Scandinavian invasion of Shetland begins in the Ice Age when the islands were over-ridden by glaciers radiating from Norway. Subsequent local glaciations deepened the valleys; the longest loch in Shetland, Loch Cliff of Unst, occupies such a trough, length 3 miles from north to south, with a long weedy leg thrusting south-east for $\frac{3}{4}$ of a mile.

The whole loch is shallow, the maximum depth being only 21 ft at the widest part, which is just over $\frac{1}{4}$ of a mile, the narrow off-shoot being less than 10 ft deep. The north end is good for sea trout, while the biggest brown trout are found in the south end, though these are unlikely to be more than 8 oz, and double that size is considered very good. Boats are available from the Springfield Hotel at 50p per day to residents and £1 to non-residents.

There is evidence in the blanket bog around Loch Cliff that trees grew here around 500 B.C. before the climate became wetter and peat began to form. Today the rainfall averages out at 45 in. which is half that of Loch Maree in Western Ross, and the peat is eroding. Despite being nearly 61° north, in the same latitude as South Greenland, snow lies on only 12 to 15 days a year and frost is of infrequent occurrence, owing to the benign influence of the Gulf Stream.

No one who goes to Unst should miss the chance of exploring Hermaness, the 3-mile peninsula projecting north of Loch Cliff where you run the gauntlet of aggressive Great and Arctic skuas in the rough ground which they defend in the breeding season, the 'Bonxies' big as buzzards giving vicious 'coughs' as they drive in for a low flying attack. More vicious are the smaller swallow-tailed Arctic skuas, dive-bombing from above, and much more liable to strike hard. The population could be 1,000 Bonxies and 150 or so Arctics – which is a big success story in protection since numbers were down to only 7 pairs of Bonxies in 1895. The RSPB maintain a watcher and Hermaness itself is a National Nature Reserve.

The cliffs, which drop to the sea west of the Warden's Hut on Hermaness Hill and continue in chaotic tenement of birds to Muckle Flugga, have been well documented since 1917 when a few pairs of gannets bred for the first time, rising to 1,000 pairs by

overleaf: Unst, the most northerly of the Shetlands

Shetlander with a sea trout

Lerwick, capital of the Shetlands

Scalloway, the former capital of the Shetlands

The Loch of Spiggie

1937, increasing to 3,000 in 1949 and to over 5,000 pairs in the next 20 years. Beginning on Vesta Skerry they gradually spread to Muckle Flugga and Hermaness pushing out guillemots and kittiwakes, as they did on Noss near Lerwick.

They repeated the success story of the fulmar which nested here in 1897 for the first time and is now abundant, together with tens of thousands of snub-nosed puffins and large kittiwake colonies. Razorbills and guillemots are scarcer. There is also a local race of moths, darker than those on the Scottish mainland, having evolved that way as a result of isolation. Amongst these Caradrinidae are the following: 'True Lovers' Knot, Northern Rustic, Autumnal Rustic, Square-spot Rustic; while the dark characteristics can also be seen in the Hydriomenidae and the Hepialidae.

The Management Plan of the Nature Conservancy on Hermaness is to perpetuate the undisturbed conditions of this fascinating place and study the bird populations and inter-relationships—important in these days when sea birds all over the world are being badly effected by pollution.

Loch of Snarravoe at the opposite end of Unst, in the south-west, is in peat-free ground and is noted for its golden trout weighing about $\frac{3}{4}$ lb. Triangular in shape and $\frac{1}{2}$ a mile at its broadest, the maximum depth is 29 ft. Loch of Stourhoull just north of the above mentioned has a reputation for large fighting fish. Loch of Watlee close to the A968 is a safe wading loch with good fishing and is the second biggest water in Unst.

Since it is impossible within the scope of one chapter to deal with all the lochs of Shetland, I am going to jump for contrast from the extreme north to Loch of Spiggie in south Mainland, in the friendly parish of Dunrossness only a few miles north of the airport of Sumburgh. Plenty of variety here, with farms, croft-lands, the big cliffs of Fitful Head, the excavated wonders of the Jarlshof, said to be one of the most remarkable sites in Britain, and St Ninian's Isle with its evidence that the Shetland Picts were converted to Christianity long before St Columba landed on Iona.

Loch of Spiggie is notable in its own right, not only for being the only large loch in south Mainland but for being the fourth largest in the Shetlands at $1\frac{1}{3}$

miles long by $\frac{1}{2}$ a mile broad, with a maximum depth of 41 ft. And it has a big reputation among fishermen, early in the season for brown trout and from late August onwards for sea trout. It contains arctic char and is so shallow in the north end that it can be waded from shore to shore, but boats are available from Henderson's Hotel and permits cost 25p per day, 75p per week or £2 for the season.

Loch of Spiggie and its surroundings of croft houses, bays, cliffs and islands is one of the best ornithological centres in Shetland with variety in plenty, from water birds including the red-necked phalarope to skuas on the moor, arctic terns on the sands to stormy petrels on the near island of Colsay. And the boat for Fair Isle leaves from Grutness Pier just south of Sumburgh Airport less than five miles distant, close to Jarlshof, which the Ministry of Works describes as one of the most remarkable archaeological sites in Britain.

What makes Jarlshof, on a green headland above a sandy beach, unique is that within 3 acres is a chronology in stone of the people who occupied this place from Bronze and Iron Age times to the Viking period, including a broch and courtyard protecting partly roofed wheelhouses, the best examples of their kind dating from the first centuries A.D.

Much in the period puzzle has still to be elucidated, between the first ovals of the stone huts, preserved in sand as at Skara Brae in Orkney, through the different structures modified by successive waves of people who re-used the stones for their own constructions. But plenty of pottery with Neolithic affinities was found. Then from the period of stone and bone implements to that of bronze swords, axes and knives, even to the smithy where they were made, with stocks of clay and the quern for preparing it.

The broch came later, to be abandoned and its stones used for other structures, one of them a large round house, which in turn became wheelhouses. Following that came the Viking foundations of the most complete settlement yet found in Britain, its growth over 2 acres revealing its evolution from the ninth to the thirteenth century, the original settlers hailing from the More-Trondelag regions of Norway, most probably. In the wheelhouse phase preceding the Vikings it would appear that Shetland was occupied by the northern Picts.

St Ninian's Isle 2 miles north of Loch of Spiggie
was the scene of exciting excavations between 1955–9
when beneath a mediaeval church was found the
ruins of a pre-Norse church and a wooden box turned
upside down. It hid a silver treasure of 12 brooches,
8 bowls and 9 other objects, one inscribed in Latin
and Pictish, valuables of the church hidden in haste,
possibly around A.D. 800. The green island is accessible
by a strand from Bigton and St Ninian's Well is still
a clear stream.

Of the total population of Shetland numbering
around 18,000 about one third live in Lerwick, a
town on a hill of sharp angles where the gable ends
of houses tower one above the other and canyons lead
between narrow walls. The flagstones paving the
main street and the constant stir of boats in Bressay
Sound give it a delightfully foreign atmosphere.

You could describe Loch of Clickhimin as being in
the suburbs, only ten minutes from Commercial Street
with a broch on a bouldery promontory to give it
character. And the Shetland folk make good use of it,
especially on the last Tuesday in January in the Fire
Festival of 'UP HELLY AA' when a specially-built
Norse dragon ship with a Guiser crew is dragged on
wheels, the shields and winged head-dress of the
warriors lit by the torchlight of the procession as they
march to Clickhimin to fire the ship in an echo of the
old Viking funeral rite of cremating the possessions
with the man. The death in this case is winter, the
return of the sun and the light, a throwback to the
Norse laws and customs which continued here until
the seventeenth century.

This is just the beginning of a night of feast and
fiesta, as teams of guisers make a night of dancing and
visiting and drinking. To be the Guiser Jarl, Chief
of the Warriors, is a great honour and the one chosen
must visit every function that is going on that wild
night, nor will anyone lay off until dawn and the
public holiday which follows. Go to Shetland then
if you would learn the Norse truth that 'Man is the
delight of man', and if you can stand the pace from
the ceremony of boarding the long ship to its burning
and the all-night revelries which follow, then you are
worthy to take your place in a festival which no
islander wants to miss. And if you go as a guiser in a

Wheel-houses of Jarlshof evolved from brochs

Jarlshof and the foundations of Norwegian 'Long House' farms

Weisdale, looking across to crofts and loch

Finding a snowy owl's nest on Fetlar

Young snowy owls on Fetlar

Fetlar

face mask, then you must remain masked until your identity is found out. But you must use your time to 'take-off' yourself, or individuals present, or produce some satire on local events. And your disguise once worn, must never be worn again.

The broch at Clickhimin was found in 1953 to be built beside the internal structures of an earlier stone fort, of a type from which the brochs evolved, dating back to the fourth and second century B.C. The excavations revealed for the first time the domestic arrangements of an early Celtic fortress by people with the same culture as the Bronze Age and Iron Age people of Jarlshof. A change of loch level, causing flooding, enforced changes in fort construction.

What seems to be accepted about the brochs from the most recent excavations is that they were the strongholds of an agricultural population of 2,000 years ago and were part of a village complex for refuge. Also, that when their use passed, they were pulled down or converted into other uses. Mousa

Midsummer midnight on Shetland

standing 40 ft high and unbroken is the best example in existence, and can be reached by boat from Sandwick, 14 miles south of Lerwick.

Loch of Clickhimin is ½ a mile long by ¼ of a mile broad, with a maximum depth of 10 ft and a mean of 5–6 ft, and although tidal, the south shore is rich in fresh-water shrimps and good brown trout are caught without wading.

Loch of Girlsta. Six miles north of Lerwick this loch contains three times as much water as any other loch in Shetland with a maximum depth of 74 ft and a mean of 31 ft in 1½ miles of length and ⅓ of a mile in breadth. Situated among heathery hills it is a true rock basin, contains char and has a reputation for big brown trout. Spinning for them is allowable here, but not elsewhere on any Association Water. Two boats are available to permit holders at the south end.

Loch of Tingwall. This fertile spot was an important place in Norse times, for it was in this attractive valley 4 miles from Lerwick that justice was meted out at a

special Lawting presided over by the Lord of Shetland or the King of Norway. Tingvallur in Iceland is held to be the place where the first 'Parliament' in the world met to govern in democratic fashion. The same principles held in Shetland. At Tingwall trial of criminals was by jury, and the guilty had their backs broken on a stone. Quarrels were sometimes solved by fighting it out in a boxing ring, on a little peninsula of Tingwall Loch when the first man to shed blood on the ground lost.

The valley preserves its air of civilization and the long loch gives excellent fishing in a charming location of green fields and rolling croftlands. The loch has six boats on it and lots of 1-lb fish and twice that weight are taken, though the average is 11 oz or so. The length is over 1 mile, the breadth $\frac{1}{4}$ of a mile, with shallows at mid-length where the depth is only 9 ft, while around the island the depth goes down to 2–3 ft.

The loch then is in two basins, the north being shallower, with a maximum depth of 40 ft though it is mostly flat bottomed and 7–9 ft deep. The southern basin is quite different, with a maximum of 60 ft in a simple rock basin whose mean is 19 ft.

Loch of Asta is almost linked to Tingwall Loch on the south and is $\frac{1}{2}$ a mile long by $\frac{1}{8}$ of a mile broad, with a mean depth of only 5 ft and a maximum of 13 ft near the north end. As well as brown trout there is a run of sea trout from East Voe.

Loch of Strom at $2\frac{1}{2}$ miles in length is one of the longest lochs in Shetland with a breadth of only $\frac{1}{3}$ of a mile and it is a rock basin into which the tide enters, but with little effect on its level. Studded with little islands, it is in two basins, whose maximum depth is 12 ft in the north and 13 ft in the south. It gets a good reputation for sea trout and grilse, especially the head of the loch.

Roer Water. This loch lies beneath Ronas Hill, the highest in the Shetlands at 1,476 ft, and a view from that top will show the impossibility of dealing with more than just a few lochs where there are so many, but as this is the largest loch in North Roe it must be mentioned.

Length $\frac{2}{3}$ of a mile by $\frac{1}{4}$ of a mile, the maximum depth is 32 ft with a mean of 10 ft and it is a rock basin, easily fished from the shore, but there is a boat

A Shetland scene

161

obtainable from Mr W Moat, Burra Voe.

There is no space left to deal with the excellent fishing lochs of Yell, second largest of the Shetlands, but I must mention Fetlar which came into the news in 1967 when a pair of snowy owls made history by nesting on Vord Hill just across the sea from Unst and Yell. This unique event brought more visitors to Fetlar in a single year than for half a century, and the the RSPB took appropriate action by mounting a telescope in a hide to enable ornithologists to see the birds with the minimum of disturbance.

I was lucky to have a face-to-face view of the white male and found myself hypnotised by the silvery eyes, pupils like black slits, staring at me, the heavy lids and furry 'nose' with jet-black tip giving it a strangely animal look – partly due to the enormous roundness of its head.

I was fascinated too by the legs, bright as those of a kestrel, but the gold colour was feathers extending down over the claws – winter warmers indeed. Rotating its head like a gun turret, it was missing nothing going on around it. Flying back to its perch, it now demonstrated how it kills its prey.

It was done by stealth. Perched just beneath the skyline like a white stone, the owl must have spotted its victim and waited for it to move out of sight. This is the only explanation for its behaviour, for now it flew low, following the contours of the ground, practically ski-ing the last few feet over a bank, to rise with a rabbit in its claws. Dead ground hid the actual strike, but I saw it standing with the prey for five minutes, then flying with it to the nest.

Nor was this the end, for the female, who hardly ever leaves the nest, got up and circled around, showing her larger proportions and browner plumage, returning to the nest to carry off a small black rabbit and drop it a short distance away. The male was not having any of this, however. He promptly dropped on the rabbit and carried it back to the nest.

I was allowed to visit the nest and see the six young, more like grey kittens than birds. Five of them flew eventually and were wintering on the island at the time of the Up Helly Aa Fire Festival – true Norsemen returned. This rate of breeding success has not been matched since, but the birds are still present at the time of writing.

Fetlar is perhaps the most fertile island of the Shetlands, and is said to have been the first to be colonised by the Norse. There are three good fishing lochs, Papil Water, Loch of Winyadepla and Loch of Funzie, the first and last named containing sea trout as well as brown trout. Permission can be obtained locally. Alas, the population of Fetlar, like all the outlying islands, is declining steadily, the present score being about a hundred, men, women and children, yet at the time when Shetland men were 'pressed' into Nelson's Navy more than 100 were removed from Fetlar into the service.

There is much to see here, from the Wick of Gruting where the Russian fishing boats lie up, to the Horn of Ramsness where the Lamb Hoga plunges into the sea. Wherever you walk you are amongst a shrilling of whimbrel, usually to a swooping accompaniment of bonxies, or by bog cotton lochans with red-throated divers in them, or maybe red-necked phalaropes. At night time you can go out to the cliffs and listen to the purring of stormy petrels.

The Shetlands may be the finest bird islands in Britain, with in addition an unrivalled assortment of fishing lochs. But it is the people who bring me back.

Puffins crowd the seaward ledges

Lochs of the Outer Hebrides

Lewis, Harris, North Uist, Benbecula, South Uist,
Eriskay and Barra

In the Highland Development Board booklet *Game
Fishing in the Outer Hebrides* author James Coutts
prefaces his chosen lochs with the words that'. . . to
list all the lochs in these islands would require a book
of telephone directory dimensions'. A look at a large
scale map is enough to show why even the energetic
men of the *Bathymetrical Survey of the Scottish Fresh-water
Lochs* baulked the task by picking only a representative
sample from Lewis, Benbecula and North Uist,
pointing out that of many hundreds of lochs of all
shapes and sizes, few are straight valley lochs and that
a great many of them are brackish.

The fertile Orkneys and the rugged and indented
Shetlands are simple compared to the contrasts of the
Western Isles, with their mountains of gneiss and
machairs of shell sand, the east side offering anchorages and harbours, the west side open to the Atlantic
and rich in pasture. Between these different worlds lie
mazes of lochs, many named, but many more unnamed.
What the Orkneys, the Shetlands and the Outer
Hebrides have in common is inexpensive and excellent
fishing easily accessible by air or sea.

You can be in Benbecula in one hour from Glasgow,
or you can take your car on the ferry from Uig in
Skye to Lochmaddy in North Uist, or go on across the
Sound of Harris to Tarbert to explore the biggest
island in Britain even if the names Lewis and Harris
makes it sound like two islands.

The Outer Islands, from Barra Head to the Butt of
Lewis is the Gaelic-speaking stronghold of Scotland
where the crofting tradition is very much alive and
much combined with weaving tweed and fishing.
Stornoway is the only town, centre of the Harris tweed
industry, with a population of 2,000 in the Burgh and
5,000 in the town. A full third of all the people in
Lewis live here, yet this is what Martin Martin wrote
in 1703: 'There is a village called Stornoway, at the
head of the bay of that name; it consists of about
sixty families; there are some houses of entertainment
in it, as also a church and school in which Latin and
English are taught.'

It has a special place in the affections of Lewismen
today for it is only here they can legally buy a glass of

whisky, yet in Martin Martin's time the industrious natives brewed several sorts of liquors, one of them four times distilled called usquebaugh. This may be the reason why the roadside verges leading out of town are littered with the empty bottles discarded by the disgusted Gaels who must travel far and drink fast when they get the chance.

Lewis is not so much a peat blanket, as a wrinkled cap enclosing water in its numerous folds. Loch Suainaval is the deepest loch, a Lewisian gneiss rock basin dropping to 219 ft. Breadth $\frac{1}{2}$ a mile maximum, there are two deep basins, one of 212 ft in this broadest part, and another containing the maximum depth just south of the centre of the loch, the overall mean depth being $108\frac{1}{2}$ ft which is three times more than that of any other loch in Lewis. Length $2\frac{2}{3}$ miles it is one of the longest lochs, with fine mountains to the west, and to the east over a ridge, Loch Grunavat now a reservoir of the North of Scotland Hydro-Electric Board.

Loch Stacsavat. This loch intervenes between Loch Suainaval and the sea, and is roughly triangular, length $\frac{3}{4}$ of a mile by $\frac{1}{3}$ of a mile with a maximum depth of 40 ft and a mean of $17\frac{1}{2}$ ft. A rock basin like its large neighbour, it discharges into one of the loveliest bays in the Hebrides at Uig Sands, a place hallowed by the find in 1831 of a set of superbly carved chessmen of walrus ivory, almost certainly Norse. They may be seen in the Scottish National Museum, Edinburgh. The finest rock climbing in Lewis can be found in the hills rising immediately south. To the east through rocky Glen Valtos lies Valtos and its magnificent bays which should not be missed. See the situation of these clustering crofts and you know why people want to live in the Hebrides. Alas, there is little in the way of accommodation here but there is no restriction on camping or caravanning.

Not very far away, at the foot of East Loch Roag are the Standing Stones of Callanish described by the unemotional Ministry of Works as 'A cruciform setting of megaliths unique in Scotland and outstanding in Great Britain'. In fact its only rival is the celebrated Stonehenge on Salisbury Plain, as was discovered in the middle of last century when $5\frac{1}{2}$ ft of peat was dug out to reveal the true height and

overleaf: Stornoway

The standing stones of Callanish on Lewis

proportions of not just a normal circle but a cross of
stones. The depth of peat had accumulated since it
was built around 1500 B.C. when the pattern of
settlement on the isles was vastly different from what
it is today if we are to judge from another seven stone
circles within a short radius of Callanish.

This stone temple must have been one of great
importance, the tallest megalith being 15 ft 6 in. high
by a cairn in the centre of a circle of 13 large stones
approached by an avenue of 19 stones, with projections
east and west of the circle to form a cross. The climate
was better and no doubt the land was more fertile
when prehistoric people built these monuments.
Today in Lewis, apart from the settlement of Achmore,
everybody lives away from the peat blanket of the
interior by the sea where the land can be worked,
though a treatment of surface seeding is winning
land from the peat.

Just to the north of Callanish above Loch an Duin

Dun Carloway, the best preserved broch in the Western Isles

is the best preserved broch in the Western Isles, Dun
Carloway, now shaped rather like a pinnacle, its
highest point 30 ft above the base with galleries within
the thick walls. This broch could be called the
culmination of dry-stone building in the Western
Isles, no doubt evolving from the simpler duns which
are so common on lochs on islands in these parts,
pre-dating the brochs. Similarly the Standing Stones
of Callanish are thought to have evolved from a simple
cairn to a stone circle and then a cross.

The Neolithic and the Iron Age people left their
memorials in stone, the Norsemen in the place names
of hills and lochs such as *Langavat*, meaning 'long
water', well named from the way it wriggles from the
Harris border into the Lochs district of Lewis, that
peat and water maze which extends from Loch Seaforth to Stornoway. Loch Langavat by its shortest
measurement is $7\frac{1}{4}$ miles of zig-zagging rock basins
excavated by the glaciers which scooped them out

Loch Seaforth and the hills of Harris

from weaker rocks. Maximum breadth $\frac{3}{4}$ of a mile, the maximum depth is 98 ft in the southern basin nearest the big hills where the loch is straight for almost 3 miles. Then it shallows to 9 ft beyond which is the mid-basin.

There is a constriction here where the loch forks north-east, soon attaining a depth of 90 ft and shallowing before another change of direction east to the third basin which is over 3 miles long, much islanded and irregular of shoreline, with a maximum depth of 65 ft. Situated remotely and difficult to comprehend from its winding shores, the best way of viewing the loch is to take the path from Vigadale Bay on Loch Seaforth and walk west for a couple of miles to a pass commanding a fine view of the head of the wild loch, whose foot is another maze of lochs stretching almost to Callanish.

Loch Benisval to the west of Langavat is another remotely situated loch and at 95 ft maximum depth

Loch More Barvas

is the third deepest in Lewis, with a mean of 35 ft which is higher than Langavat, though the length is only ¾ of a mile by ½ a mile, the form being a rough oblong with a little protruding tail end. It takes its name from the peak Benisval rising 350 ft above it and shelving steeply into it.

Loch More Barvas is an example of a very different kind of Hebridean loch, a shallow sheet of water ponded by shell sand on grassy machair with crofting fields sloping down to its shores, with a short salmon river running from it into the sea. A mile long from east to west and ½ a mile broad, the mean depth is only 4½ ft with a maximum of 8 ft, nothing more than a sandbar separating it from the sea where seals lurk to poach salmon, and are shot at by the jealous onlookers waiting to net the running fish. Like many of the best lochs in Lewis, waters are preserved, but there is plenty of good free and inexpensive fishing round Stornoway.

Salmon netting on the short river between Loch More Barvas and the sea

Among some lochs which may be fished free of charge near Stornoway are the following:

Loch Airigh nan Gleann $3\frac{1}{2}$ miles south of the town and good for trout.

Loch Beag a' Ghrianain lies adjacent to above and is recommended.

Mar a' Ghrianain in the same neighbourhood, smallish trout.

Loch Breugach 5 miles from Stornoway, boats available, enquire at Ship Chandler R Morrison, 5 Bank St, Stornoway. Trout are said to be big.

Loch Beag na Craoibhe, adjacent to above named, small trout but plenty of them.

Loch Leiniscall (Ghost Loch). Near the above named, slightly larger fish than na Craoibhe.

Loch a' Bhuna and Loch an Eilein on the Stornoway-Uig road 6 miles from the town, and Loch Mar a' Chocair and Loch Vatandip on the Stornoway–Pentland Road are also recommended.

Harris is less Norse in place names, no doubt because the high hills left less scope for settlement. The population today is around 3,000, and the old truism that the finest scenery makes the poorest agriculture is very much in evidence, especially around the Clisham and the weird peaks of Strone Ulladale in the forest of Harris – meaning deer forest for this is very much sporting territory.

A walk *par excellence* I would recommend is from Amhuinnsuidhe on the Husinish road north by Loch Chliostair following on past Loch Ashavat to look at the overhanging snout of Strone Ulladale now offering Dolomitic challenge to the new breed of artificial climbers as they force mechanised ways up it.

The great crag looks as if it was in the act of falling but the rock is gneiss, polished and hard, and under the threatening beak lies Glen Ulladale broken by a loch of the same name. By cutting east a keen walker can return by adjacent Glen Meavaig in a longish but not too strenuous expedition. Loch Chliostair is a reservoir now with a spillway level at 542 ft for hydro-electricity, length nearly 1 mile by $\frac{1}{3}$ of a mile broad. For exploring this region I recommend the grassy machair of Husinish which is ideal for camping with nothing to block the view at the tip of the peninsula where the road ends across from the Isle of Scarp. The white sands here are amongst the finest in the Hebrides. They are rivalled only by the Traigh Luskentyre across West Loch Tarbert.

Tarbert is the car ferry terminal for Harris, the route being via North Uist, with a connection from there to Skye. Tarbert means a narrow neck of land dividing water, and the narrowness of the constriction here almost makes two islands of North and South Harris. The hotel has the fishing in Laxdale lochs just 2 miles east, with boats and ghillie available at around £2 per day. Good catches of sea trout and salmon are taken. Laig Guest House has the fishing on Loch Aidh.

There are good fishings which can be arranged with Horsacleit Estate who have two lodges sleeping six, to let at £50 per week including ghillie. Day tickets on their group of lochs can also be had from Mrs A Y Jamieson, Invercarse Harris. For lodge renting inquire to Mrs W D Bertram, 26 Collington Road, Edinburgh 10, telephone 031–447 6813.

Magnificent fishing can also be had from Borve

Estate who control a large area of excellent lochs holding salmon, sea trout and brown trout. Unfortunately, they are often let for the whole season, but an inquiry to the Factor, Borve Lodge Cottage, Scarista, Harris will obtain the necessary information.

South Harris is two different worlds, curving with sands and grasslands to the west, and carved out of rocks on the east where the soil has to be scraped together and built up into lazybeds to grow tiny patches of oats and potatoes. But the little bays make good anchorages for lobster boats, and descendants of people dispossessed from better land continue to live the old way. In the small rectangle of South Harris there is every kind of Hebridean landscape, ending at the southern tip with the early sixteenth-century church of St Clement, described by the Ministry of Works as being '. . . the only church of a monumental character in the outer isles'. Ornate in architectural detail, it is an appropriate masterpiece with which to leave, and cross the Sound of Harris to North Uist out of whose 12 by 16 miles 8,000 acres is fresh-water, and 20,000 acres foreshore and tidal waters.

To capture the flavour of North Uist it is only necessary to take a sip, not drink the whole bottle, for no more bewildering region of lochs exists in Britain. Take Loch Scadavay, so labyrinthine in its maze that although the length is only $4\frac{1}{4}$ miles by 2 miles broad, the shore-line is 50 miles – a ratio of circumference to length unequalled by any other loch. Yet it is so beset with islands that there is no extent of open water visible, and while the maximum depth is 50 ft, the mean is a mere 9 ft. Containing one island nearly a mile long, while others have ancient dun fortifications reached by submerged causeways, it is not unrepresentative of the lochs straggling in such confusion down the east side of North Uist and nearly encircling Eaval – Ey Fjall to give it its Norse name, which means Island Hill because it is so nearly cut off. So to climb the highest hill you almost need a boat to reach the 1,138-ft top.

An easier sip however, if you would have a golden eagle's view of North Uist, is to go north out of Lochmaddy by car or bicycle and climb the 625 ft of Ben Mhor opposite Harris. Only by getting up can you appreciate the hidden contrasts of this flat land, not only the dramatic differences between east and west, but realise the magnitude of desert sands and watery topography spread out before you in an extraordinary map drawn in relief and coloured by sky and sea.

Westward stretch the great sands, mile upon curving mile, ridged inland by dunes and becoming floral pastures, the machair lands where the township cattle graze in large herds, joyous with birds and flowers in summer, in winter provided with great tangles of weed, blown in on Atlantic gales for fertilising the fields. Lochmaddy is on the east side because of the harbour and shelter opposite Skye where the car ferry operates. But the life of North Uist is the machair lands where townships like Tighgarry, Houghgarry and Paible send up their peat reek. Other townships are on tidal islands or out on Bernera. The population has dropped from 5,000 in 1821 to the more reasonable figure of 1,800 now, though the impression you may get if you keep to the main road is of an almost deserted island, for the crofts and most delightful bays lie off it.

The Tourist Office in Lochmaddy will give you some addresses if you are looking for accommodation, and if you are an angler temporarily resident on the island it costs only 75p to join the North Uist Angling Club and get the right to fish by fly a big variety of waters from the bank. Permits for those North Uist Estate fishings outwith Club waters are obtainable from the Manager, Loch Maddy Hotel, Isle of North Uist, telephone Lochmaddy 331. Salmon fishing with a boat included is £3·50 per day, and brown trout fishing with boat £1 per day, services of a ghillie £3 per day.

Salmon waters with boats include Lochs nan Geireann, Skealtar and Ciste. Sea trout, Lochs Oban na Fiadh, Dusary, Horisary, Grogarry, na Clachan and Geireann Mill. Brown trout lochs with boats, Lochs Strumore, Scadavay, a' Bharpa, Tormasad, Eaval, Hosta and Obisary.

Loch Obisary which half encircles the highest peak, Eaval, is the largest loch by volume in North Uist and at 151 ft is twice as deep as Loch a' Glinne-Dorcha, the second deepest, though the mean depth of the latter is higher. Loch Obisary is so complex that it has fifteen rock basins. One of its islands even has a small lochan. Crescent shaped with a length of

overleaf: Outer island lochscape North Uist. From Ben Mhor southwards to Lochmaddy

3 miles along its axis, the greatest breadth is 1 mile, though the presence of islands reduces the extent of open water to half that amount. The deepest basin is between Eilean Mor and the burn running north into Loch Eport. Some of the other basins are 51, 57, 50, 65 and 58 ft deep. Like many another loch in North Uist it is affected by tides, rendering the deeper water salty and enabling marine and fresh-water organisms to overlap. When it was tested for temperature by the Bathymetric surveyors the temperature was found to be one degree lower at 50 ft than at the bottom, an interesting example of a temperature inversion.

Loch an Duin is an example of a different kind of brackish loch, fresh at one end and salt at the other, mostly shallow in its squiggling expansions, but reaching 35 ft deep in the north though the mean is 6 ft. Nearly 1 mile long and $\frac{2}{3}$ of a mile broad, the name comes from 3 duns – stone fortifications – and the broch of Dun Torcuill whose walls are 10 ft high and the best-preserved on the island. A very little rise in sea-level would reduce the brackish and fresh-water lochs of North Uist drastically. It has happened before, for undoubtedly the great east coast inlets of Loch Eport and Loch Maddy were once fresh-water lochs, and in those times North Uist must have been a much more extensive island without peat.

North Uist not only has more earth houses than elsewhere in the Hebrides, showing early settlement, but on Eilein an Tighe of Loch nan Geireann were found pottery kilns belonging to Neolithic times, probably using local birch woods for charcoal, a local industry predating the Iron Age. Fragments of pottery show that the primitive potters were highly skilled. In this complicated country the archaeologist among the lochs has much still to discover. A coin of Constantius II has been found at Vallay with house-hold utensils which, thanks to the coin, can be dated to the fourth century.

Loch an Duin is on the Newton Estate which controls the other half of the angling on North Uist and their territory is in the wilder country north of the A865. The Department of Agriculture and Fisheries for Scotland deal with enquiries from their office at Balivanich, telephone Benbecula 346. There is a wide range of fishing at modest cost, and some of the lochs quoted are as follows:

Loch an Duin, brown trout, 38p per day plus 25p with boat.
Loch na Ceardaich and Dead Man's Loch, 25p per day, brown trout.
Loch Fada, 25p per day. One boat available at 15p per day, brown trout.
Loch nan Geadh and Loch Tergavat, as above but bank fishing only, brown trout.
Loch Vergavat, brown trout as above.
Loch Traigh Ear, 50p per day.

Wildlife and the Uists are synonymous, and these islands may seem strange places to find bird sanctuaries, but the building of connecting roads and car ferries meant a steep rise in tourist traffic, so the Royal Society for the Protection of Birds with the co-operation of landowners and crofters established 1,500 acres of reserve at Balranald on the north-west tip of North Uist to safeguard marsh birds like the red-necked phalarope which needs shallow water and marshes for feeding and breeding.

Balranald is just this kind of nutrient-rich marsh with plenty of wildfowl food plants, as well as having an Atlantic beach, sand dunes, floral machair and Loch nam Feithean for waterfowl. Here is a list of some of the birds which breed, or have bred here: little grebe, mallard, teal, gadwall (probably), wigeon, shoveller, tufted duck, pochard, eider, red-breasted merganser, shelduck, mute swan, water rail, corncrake, moorhen, coot, oystercatcher, lapwing, ringed plover, red-necked phalarope, snipe, common sandpiper, redshank, dunlin, common gull, black-headed gull, common tern, arctic tern, little tern, cuckoo, skylark, hooded crow, wren, wheatear, sedge warbler, meadow pipit, rock pipit, starling, twite, corn bunting, reed bunting, house sparrow and tree sparrow – a total of 43 species – not to mention wintering species such as geese and whooper swans.

There are also Atlantic seals breeding on the little island of Causamul which is inside the reserve. The reserve is wardened and visitors wanting to learn about the birds should contact the RSPB representative at nearby Houghgarry crofting township.

From North Uist you drive across a strand to Benbecula on a good road, or you can fly direct there from Glasgow or Stornoway. Balivanich is the airport and despite the general flatness, the division between machair on the west and moorland to the east is very much the same as on North Uist, nor are the lochs any easier to grasp. They are just as irregular and bouldery, the longest being Langavat, just over 2 miles long but a mere tenth of a mile in mean breadth, maximum depth 34 ft and mean 8 ft. It is a rock basin almost cut in half by a canal 5 ft deep, and its islands are elongated along the strike of the Lewisian gneiss.

On this abnormally windy island live men of the South Uist rocket range who, if they were here long enough, would no doubt stoop like the islanders from the effects of the unrelenting blast. Shelter there is none, except perhaps on the steep curve of Culla Bay on the west coast where the Highland chief Clanranald wisely built his house though he threw caution aside in joining Bonny Prince Charlie to find himself alone, unsupported by other island chiefs. The grey stones at Nunton still defy the winds of the pancake isle whose highest hill is Rueval projecting like a pyramid in the middle of nothing.

I liked W H Murray's description of the view from the summit, with Benbecula looking 'like a well-fired crumpet pitted with holes by the hundred'. The holes of course are lochs, and beneath the top there is a famous cave where the Prince hid, waiting for Flora MacDonald to come back from Clanranald's house with the fancy dress which would enable him to escape dressed as Betty Burke. The whole world knows the story of the escape to Skye, but few people know the cave on the 'Mountain of the Fords' – the literal description of the name Benbecula.

The 'North Ford' leading to North Uist, and the 'South Ford' leading to South Uist are tamed by bridge and causeway now, making it all too easy to clear out of Benbecula whereas, not so long ago, crossing the dangerous strands called for skill and cunning, knowledge of the tides and weather. Ironically it was the easier crossing of the South Ford which cost the most lives, because people took it more casually, whereas the longer difficulties of the North Ford and its quicksands commanded more respect and care.

Creagorry Hotel is the recommended centre of fishing on Benbecula, controlling a number of lochs and able to arrange private fishing. The South Uist Angling Club also has waters on the island at a £1 per week fishing fee. There are so many lochs to choose from that it is not worth mentioning specific names, though West Loch Olavat is highly spoken of, not to mention sea trout fishing in the sea pools.

Leaving Benbecula for South Uist with no very clear destination in mind I asked the driver of the bus to let me off at what he considered to be the best place on the island. He had no hesitation at dropping me off at a road end leading to Dremisdale. It was only afterwards I discovered that he lived there, recommendation indeed. In fact he had chosen the place I would have chosen myself had I known enough, with the National Nature Reserve of Loch Druidibeg to hand and tracks running in all directions across the green machair busy with crofters. Eastward rose a different country, dark hills of nearly 2,000 feet, rocky, rough and indented with sea lochs.

The difference between North Uist and here is that the continuous string of lochs which make this the anglers' paradise of the Western Isles are on the west side on the rich sandy soil. Fishermen become poetic when they talk about South Uist. The Queen was fishing here shortly after I left. You can sail from Mallaig direct to Lochboisdale and centre yourself in this little 'Capital', or take your chance of 'Bed and Breakfast' or stay at the Ben Mor Guest House, Howmore near Dreimisdale.

Lochboisdale Hotel charges £45 a week for two rods with a boat on the outstanding salmon and sea trout lochs of Fada, Roag, Schoolhouse and Castle. Trout fishing is free to guests and is described by Mr James Coutts in *Game Fishing in the Outer Hebrides* as '. . . the best value available anywhere'. Day tickets when available can be had from Mr Hamish MacIntyre, the Factor, Benbecula and South Uist Estate Office, Askernish, South Uist.

The sandy machair sprinkled with lochs, and even bearing a golf course and a rocket firing range, is the greatest extent of it in Scotland, stretching 20 miles as a broad Atlantic fringe against the South Uist hills. This is where the majority of the people live, in little townships a mile or two off the main road. The population is 2,500, Roman Catholics in the north, Protestants in the south, and like Lewis and Harris you can often hear the clack of looms sounding from

overleaf : Lazy-bed agriculture

weaving sheds beside the croft though some men work together in little tweed mills.

A crofter-weaver here may look after cattle and 40 acres of land as well as weave four tweeds a week. An old woman gathering potatoes in a field told me she was eighty years old and apologised for her poor English. When Martin Martin wrote about South Uist in the seventeenth century he wrote of somebody nearly twice as old, a man getting past 130 and who '. . . still retains his appetite and understanding,' but had apparently retired from active work three years earlier!

It has been said that South Uist folk seldom step into a boat. They are orientated on the good calcareous machair land raising good cattle and crops. Nothing backward there. The tractor is the maid of work, but harvesting is a communal affair and it is a cheery sight to see old and young, men and women dotting the long length of the coast. The soil being light and sandy, supporting mats of flowers rather than grass, it needs a lot of rain to produce good crops and keep the pasture succulent. The machair, they say, changes its colour three times a year as succeeding waves of flowers take over. The township cattle feed as a communal herd.

The Howmore river is the most famous stream in the Outer Hebrides for monster sea trout, but owing to drought when I was there the keeper was spending his time carrying up baths of salmon and sea trout stranded in the lower pools, some of the trout weighing up to 14 lbs. He reckoned the fish were in such poor condition that they had nothing like their usual fight left in them. 'You can pull them in like cod,' he said. However the rain came that night, and round Loch a' Machair at dusk fishermen stood glorying in it, listening to the crying of whimbrel and golden plover wheeling with a vast flock of lapwings.

Grey-lag geese were on the move too, birds that had bred on the scrubby islands of the inland lochs though the gaggle of about 20 birds was only a third of the breeding population, for this is their main nesting ground in Britain, hence the reason why Loch Druidibeg has the status of a National Nature Reserve, thanks to the co-operation of crofters and the South Uist Estates. The total area is 4,145 acres, about half of which is owned by the Nature Conservancy. The reserve, comprising grass and heather moor, lochs with islands and sanddunes, shore and machair lies within the crofting townships of Dremisdale and Stilligarry. It is a perfect example of an unspoiled Hebridean system, of fertile and infertile land and water.

In describing the Loch Druidibeg Nature Reserve you have a fragment that will do for a general description of the topography of South Uist west side, with the highest point on the ground a mere 100 ft above sea-level and the deeply indented Loch Druidibeg with its many islets and peninsulas a mere 15 ft above high water. Man-made channels connect it through other lochs to the Howmore River, making Castle Loch, Loch Rigarry, Loch Stilligarry and Loch a' Machair a continuous network.

These sluggish outlet streams of Druidibeg giving out on the grassy machair and lochs with interconnecting streams beloved of birds are separated from the pebble and sand beach by dunes, the whole on a bed rock of Lewisian gneiss much grooved by the scraping of the glaciers which over-rode them. May is the sunniest month, June the driest, but the wind can blow all the time, making the temperature feel lower and the rain wetter, though in fact neither is extreme. Rainfall is a mere 50 in., and records show that the difference in mean temperature between summer and winter is around 9°F. which is small compared to most places. The wind of course is a great aid to agriculture by raising the evaporation rate which means good drying at harvest time. The prone and distorted trees of the small plantation on the reserve show the debit side of the wind factor.

Only the islands on the loch carry natural scrub, birch, rowan, willow, juniper, bramble and wild rose with a fine mixture of herbs and ferns and lots of moss. The water itself is not rich in mineral content, but the islands give security to the adult pairs of geese, while the fertile machair lochs provide the goslings with food once they hatch and are taken down there by the parent birds. Conservation would be impossible without the nurseries as well as the breeding loch, hence the nature reserve agreement with the crofters who love the birds. Herons also breed on an island here, while on the machair there are good tern colonies. Brown trout and sea trout enter the loch from the Howmore River to spawn at the eastern end where the fast flowing streams from the hills enter.

Peat stacking by Loch Erisort

Loch a' Machair

The duns on two of the islands on Druidibeg show that prehistoric man needed fortifications here; one of them, Dun Raouill, is the best preserved in South Uist, with walls over 8 ft at their thickest in a length of 71 ft by 42 ft in rectangular plan. This is unusual in type, and there is fine stonework within dividing it into two rooms. Access can be obtained by Nature Conservancy dinghy by contacting the Warden at Stilligarry, but restrictions on access to the reserve are in force between April and June when the geese are breeding.

It is worth following the maze of Druidibeg's channels east and continuing on to Loch Skiport to where half a dozen families live by lobstering and seaweed gathering, with a pier and a good harbour facing out to Skye. There is even a well-stocked shop in this once busy place, for it was from here in cattle droving days that the beasts were loaded on to schooner-rigged vessels holding perhaps fifty, to be landed at Loch Dunvegan in Skye. From there they were walked to the Crieff market after swimming the narrows at Kyle Rhea to gain the Scottish mainland.

Today there is still a good cattle trade, but the buyers come to Uist and the auction is carried out at Lochboisdale. There is also a bigger emphasis on sheep than in the old days with crofters clubbing together and dividing up the profit from the communal herd. A little museum has been opened at the north-west tip of South Uist above the maze of shallow Loch Bee, worth a visit if you want some idea of what life was like in the old days. It is situated fairly close to the Rocket Range. An impressive madonna in sparkling granite stands on the hill here.

The coming of sheep to South Uist certainly spelt bad times for the people for there was a mass of evictions to make way for them. The population then was double what it is now, and many of the evicted settled on Eriskay in these bad times of the mid-nineteenth century. Eriskay of course was the place where the *Le Dutillet* landed Prince Charlie's party on Scottish soil in the bay known as Coilleag a Phrionnsa, the 'Prince's Beach', only a short hop from South Uist. It was next day he sailed again to Loch nan Uamh to raise the clans.

However there is another little island still nearer South Uist called Calvay to which toasts are drunk for non-Jacobite reasons, for here it was that 20,000 cases of whisky were delivered up to the men of the Isles in February 1941 by the providential foundering of a ship *en route* to America with such a cargo, and the whisky was the sweetest that ever passed the lips of man. Compton Mackenzie has told the story in *Whisky Galore*. And it is the story of one landing that never did anybody any harm.

Barra, where Compton Mackenzie got his inspiration, is only a short distance from Eriskay. This Roman Catholic island has its own air service and Cockle Strand for the planes to land on, a lively place of over 1,300 people with a main centre at Castlebay, stronghold of the chief of the MacNeils. The story of this island from the great days of the herring fishing to the present would take a chapter to itself, but it could not be justified for its fishing lochs are few and space is getting short.

The Barra lochs which can be fished at 25p per day are as follows: Lochs na Cartach, an Duin, na Faolainn, St Clair and nic Ruaidhe. Lochs for which charges are quoted on application are na Doirlinn, Ard, Iosal, an Rodha, Tangasdale and several hill burns. Craigard Hotel, Castlebay, deals with applications. All are said to contain good fighting trout and some of them occasional sea trout and salmon. Bicycles are available for hire and with 14 miles of good ring road are well worth riding. In summer a boat trip should be made to Mingulay to see its thronging birds and spectacular cliffs.

Lochs of Skye
Loch Coruisk and the Storr Lochs

It is paradoxical that it is tourism which keeps the
crofting system alive in Skye, since it is the tiny fields
and the linear pattern of the whitewashed houses
which give such an alpine feel to sea-level communities dominated by the most abrupt peaks in
Britain – the Cuillin. Look from the crofts of Elgol
across the water to that eye-catching crest of 20 rock
peaks. See how they are linked one to another in a
continuous spine impossible to traverse except by
rock climbing. Over there 3,000 feet below the highest
serrations lies the 'Corrie of the Waters' – Coruisk –
carved from the naked gabbro in a rock basin without
parallel in Scotland.

You can sail to it from Elgol in summer; there are
daily fishing boat trips to the landing at Loch
Scavaig. A short walk up the outlet stream and you
are there. Far better, however, to walk the shore path
by the 'Bad Step'. The track, easy to find, begins in
the township, half way up the hill, a grassy path
running along the side of Ben Cleat and gradually
dropping to thread the sea-cliffs. Keep your mind on
your feet and stop if you want to look at arctic terns
flickering on sea-swallow wings or watch eiders or
red-breasted mergansers in the little bays below.

The crofters graze their cattle here. Look out for
the bull loaned by the Department of Agriculture for
the summer. A favourite grazing place is the big sandy
bay just before Camusunary. Over the greensward
rise the exciting contrasts between the Red Cuillin
in pink granite and the Black Cuillin in grey gabbro.
There is a shooting lodge here, and an easier but not
so interesting way to reach this point is by motor
track from Strathaird on Loch Slapin.

Round the bay and over the river by suspension
bridge the true wilderness begins as Sgurr na Stri
rises ever more steeply and the path rises to a rocky
notch, beyond which are bare gabbro slabs dotted
with erratic blocks like curling stones where the melt-
ing glaciers stranded them. The 'Bad Step' lies just
ahead where a curling rock slab goes straight into the
sea. A little islet is a useful landmark for the place.

It is no more than an easy scramble, and a way of
avoiding it has been marked with white paint on the
rocks. The alternative route was marked because so

Loch Coruisk

Skye, crofting beneath Blaven

many people get into trouble here. In fact the 'Bad Step' by any approach is no harder than the alternative. To cross the 'Bad Step' from the south, the important thing is not to keep too high. The beginning is obvious for the rock makes a pavement, from which you step on to an inclined slab split by a convenient crack in the form of a natural gangway. This crack gradually ascends to holdless rock but you have to break off leftward about half way along. In other words keep your traverse low, and don't be misled by the right forking crack. Go left easily and you strike a comfortable shelf leading to heather. The route is much easier to find coming from the opposite direction (north).

To avoid the 'Bad Step' you follow the 'Diversion' arrows by striking straight uphill for a couple of hundred feet, traverse a heathery ledge, then strike down again. A short distance on through more rocks and you are at Coruisk, whose only urbanisation is a mountain hut and a collapsed footbridge. If possible you should take yourself right round the head of the loch to savour its savagery of bog and rock. The circuit will occupy up to two hours.

That pioneer physicist J D Forbes of Pitsligo did some useful thinking when he walked here, pondering on how ice masses moved in this rock basin. He it was who discovered that the middle of a glacier moves faster than its sides, and that the upper portions move faster than the lower. An alpinist, he applied what he saw in Norway and Switzerland to formulate theories and stimulate research in Scotland. At Coruisk he saw how the abrasion and plucking effect of the moving ice had given a smooth effect to the rocks when you looked downhill, reversed when you looked up-valley to their plucked ragged edges. Forbes, who died in 1868, had foresight years ahead of his time.

Coruisk is $1\frac{3}{4}$ miles long with a maximum breadth of just over $\frac{1}{4}$ of a mile and one of its attractive features is the little islets where terns nest. There is also a fine echo to heighten the wild cries of greenshank and red-throated diver or the hoarse alarm cries of peregrine falcons. There is enough rock to make the walking surprisingly good, though camping is difficult because of the bogs. The midges are amongst the most ferocious in Scotland.

I can find no record of Loch Coruisk having been surveyed for depth. Nor is it easy to find details about

Approaching the 'Bad Step' on the Loch Coruisk path

fishing, for there is a strict security imposed by the
owner. Undoubtedly, however, it provides excellent
sea trout fishing with a few salmon, and netting used
to be done at the outflow into Loch Scavaig. The
passes leading from Coruisk into Glen Sligachan and
Glen Brittle are 'musts' for any lover of mountain
walking. And the views of Coruisk from these high
points are outstanding.

The tertiary basalt country of the Storr is quite the
opposite of sterile Loch Coruisk. Here in Trotternish
in the north of Skye the weird pinnacles of rotten
rock rise from garden-like turf cropped by sheep and
rabbits. The basalt is friable but base-rich in minerals
on which alpine plants thrive – roseroot, globe
flowers, saxifrages of several kinds, alpine ladies'
mantle, holly fern, white rock cress and one special

Crossing the 'Bad Step' which leads to the easy gangway

to this place found nowhere else in Britain, *Koenigia islandica*, the Iceland purslane.

The Storr is a collapsed mass of basalt worn into a confusion of volcanic pinnacles, the 'Old Man' tilted as if about to fall, while others are worn so thin that holes of daylight gape through them. The 'Old Man' is 160 ft high and has been climbed by two improbable routes, the first in 1955, the second in 1969. The pioneer ascent was by Don Whillans, later to distinguish himself on Annapurna by the south-west face.

A 600-ft cliff lies above these pinnacles giving out on a plateau which can be reached easily by traversing northward to avoid the rocks. From the top you can look north-west on the coast at Uig Bay where Flora Macdonald landed with the Prince in his disguise as her maid Betty Burke. Remember we left them at Benbecula trying to escape to Skye. With good weather and visibility you will see Benbecula too and be able to trace the route.

On the east side of the Storr beneath the high road lie the Storr Lochs, now forming one reservoir behind 170 ft of gravity dam 36 ft high, the water being led through 2,800 ft of tunnel to a power station on the sea-edge below. Producing 7,000,000 units a year, the spillway level is 456 ft, the combined length of the lochs being just over $2\frac{1}{2}$ miles by $\frac{1}{2}$ a mile broad.

Five boats are available for brown trout fishing on the Storr Lochs, permits from Macdonald & Fraser, Solicitors, National Bank Buildings, Portree, telephone Portree 39. The cost varies from £1·25 in May to £1·50 in August and September. The best catch of recent years however was a fossil lizard of seventy million years ago, 10 feet of vertebrae proving it to be Ichthyosaurus. You can see the rock impression of it in the Royal Scottish Museum, Edinburgh. Another interesting find near here was some tenth-century silver and some Samarkand coins, the loot of a far travelled Norseman who finished up here no doubt when this was Viking land. The Norse place names remain.

Before leaving this part of the world a visit should be made to the Quirang above the crofts of Staffin, another weird place of slipped basalt worn into fantastic shapes and rich with wild flowers. A track

The easy gangway above Loch Coruisk

leads in from Loch Langaig, a neat gem like so many lochans in Skye.

Lochs of interest to fishermen by permit are as follows:

Loch	Trout	Hotel	Per Day
Bernisdale	Brown	Skeabost	£1·05
Claigan	Brown and Sea	Dunvegan	50p
Connan	Brown	Ullinish Lodge	£1
Duagrich	Brown	Ullinish Lodge	£1
Ravag	Brown	Ullinish Lodge	£1

The rock basin of Loch Coruisk

The 'Old Man of Storr' above the Storr lochs

Lochs of Mull
Loch Frisa and Loch Ba

Mull, like Skye, is much indented by the sea and rich in variety but has only two notable fresh-water lochs, both of them fairly close to Salen, north and south of the short neck which separates Loch na Keal and the Sound of Mull; Loch Frisa in an open valley, Loch Ba pushing into a ring of fine peaks which close its head.

Loch Frisa was the scene of some of the first measuring work tried by the Bathymetric Survey of Sir John Murray and Fred Pullar but the results were never published because the plumbing instrument proved untrustworthy, so they designed a new machine called the Pullar Sounding Machine which is still in use at the Loch Lomond Field Station after 70 years of splendid work.

The new machine showed Loch Frisa to be in 3 separate 150-ft basins separated from each other by shallower water, the deepest where the loch is widest in the middle of the loch, being 205 ft deep. Fast moving ice dug these basins in the tertiary volcanic rock, the openness of the valley assisting the process. Length $4\frac{1}{2}$ miles by just over $\frac{1}{2}$ a mile, its north-west–south-east orientation is exactly the same as Loch Ba, though the outlets are at opposite ends. Large scale forestry has been changing the upper shores of Loch Frisa since 1925.

Loch Frisa and Loch Ba, including their rivers, are covered by the same fishing permits costing £2 per rod per day and £5 per week, for trout, sea trout and salmon. The Manager, Killiechronan Office, Aros; telephone Aros 54, deals with applications. Loch Ba is 3 miles long and $\frac{3}{4}$ of a mile broad with a maximum depth of 144 ft in its widest portion to the north. It is a rock basin in granophyre whose water level has been heightened by a dam of raised beach material at the outlet. There are fine natural oakwoods on the south shore and a good track for walking, with shapely peaks rising in a horseshoe round the head. Two good hill paths cross the range from Loch Ba, one by Glen Clachaig over the shoulder of Ben More – a notable view point. The one from the head of the loch joins with Glen More further east.

Mull is made up of great terraces of volcanic rock which break down to good soil, their greensward in

places like Balmeanach smooth as carpets under dark
headlands, a landscape spattered with cattle and
fronted by islands, Ulva, Staffa and the Treshnish.
The good car ferry service from Oban is opening up
its charms. Second of the Inner Hebrides after Skye,
it is a place to explore.

Tobermory, the attractive capital of Mull

overleaf 200/201: The mountains of Mull

overleaf 202/203: Terraces of volcanic rock at Balmeanach, Mull

Lochs of the Galloway Highlands

*Lochs Trool, Valley, Neldricken, Arron, Long Loch and
Round Loch of Glenhead, Enoch, Twachtan, Macaterick,
Fanny, Finlas, Derclach, Riecawr, Goosie, Ballochling,
Gower, Muck, Doon, Kendoon, Carsfad, Earlston, Round
and Long Loch of Dungeon, Clatteringshaws, Ken, Girvan's
Eye, Cornish, Skelloch, Lure, Bradan and Brecbowie*

Here in south-western Scotland is an outcrop of
the Highlands, a combination of Trossachs and
Cairngorms in a sudden outcropping of granite
between the Clyde and the Solway, where the turfy
farmlands swell behind Girvan to a rocky hinterland
of lochs and glens before dropping in another green
apron to Wigtown Bay. The best of it belongs to Glen
Trool Forest Park which is the largest of its kind in
Scotland, and it has never been easier to explore,
thanks to a network of forest tracks which penetrate
from all directions, notably around the head of
Loch Trool.

Loch Trool is one of the great scenic transformations
of Galloway. Following the River Cree north from
Newton Stewart among yellow reed beds and green
foothills of cattle and sheep you swing east in 8 miles
to face a sudden rise of Trossachs-style country. It is
unmistakably the Highlands, yet Loch Trool is only
250 ft above high tide level, so the steep hills have a
scale of grandeur out of all proportion to their true
height.

Yet it is perhaps the change of colour which makes
the greatest impact, the sudden feast of bronze, reds,
and yellows, reminiscent of Loch Katrine in autumn.
But the spring comes earlier here, with a rush of
flowers as the oaks break bud, and happy the person
who has a tent or caravan at Loch Trool then in the
delightful clearings of the natural forest which make
this one of the finest camp sites in Scotland. And there
is lots of room and privacy, thanks to the imaginative
way the sites have been laid out.

Deciduous woods fringe the narrow road all the
way up the loch, screening the thick mats of sitka
spruce and larch. The road ends at Bruce's Stone and
now you are on the fringe of the Cairngorm country,
except that there are more lochs hidden in that
granite cauldron than in the Cairngorms, some
draining to the Clyde and some to the Solway. The
spattered lochans occupy what was once a great

reservoir of ice like Rannoch Moor, and Loch Trool—at your feet—is a rock basin dug by one of the masses of ice which drained the cauldron.

The floor of the loch has been carved into three basins, the deepest at the eastern end where the steep hillsides flatten out in a depth of 55 ft below water, then shallowing to 24 ft, deepening again in the mid-basin to 48 ft, shoaling again to another barrier covered by only 12 ft of water, then sinking in the third basin to 36 ft.

The total length of the slightly curved loch is roughly $1\frac{1}{2}$ miles, with the broadest part at $\frac{1}{4}$ of a mile east of the Maiden Isle opposite Bruce's Stone. It was on the far side of the loch Bruce ambushed an English force by rolling stones down on them from above— a victory that was to lead to the success of Bannockburn and the return of Galloway to Scotland. Just 200 years before Bruce the Viking rule which had lasted for 300 years was coming to its end. The place names today are derived from Norse and Gaelic, as in the Rig of Jarkness, where 'Rig' is Norse for 'ridge' and 'Jarkness' comes from the Gaelic 'Uachness', meaning 'lonely desolate waste'.

No fishing is permitted in Loch Trool, but anglers who enjoy a walk will find a wealth of free fishing in the upper lochs by following up the hanging valley of the Gairland torrent to the staircase of lochs which feed Loch Trool. The lowest in this series is Loch Valley at 1,050 ft, and the highest Loch Arron at 1,450 ft with Loch Neldricken in between at 1,146.

Loch Valley is a trout loch a mile long and much indented by bays on its north shore, fed to the east by the slightly higher Loch Narroch. Loch Neldricken discharges into it in half a mile of short turbulent stream. Both lochs are about the same size and nearly equal in sinuosity, except that Neldricken is nearly cut in two by a peninsula projecting from the north, while just west of it is the strange cut-off known as the 'Murder Hole' of S R Crockett's fiction story *The Raiders*. The Galloway novelist has given a sinister atmosphere to the place.

In fact it is a cheery place by reason of the rocky character of Craignaw whose granite rises above the east shore and breaks down into silver sand edging the lagoons. True the hollow is marshy and the stream

overleaf: Loch Trool

A corner of Loch Trool camp and caravan park

The Bruce Stone, Loch Trool

from the 'Murder Hole' leads up to Loch Arron, which, tiny as it is, has its bay of granite sand beneath the Nick of the Dungeon, 'Nick' meaning 'neck', an exciting pass into the Dee Valley.

On the return journey you could link the other two Trool lochs by crossing the bouldery Rig of Jarkness to the Long Loch and the Round Loch of Glenhead which are 960 ft and 980 ft respectively above sea-level. These lochs are only 200 yds apart but occupy separate rock basins, the marshy Long Loch under Jarkness and the Round Loch under Craiglee.

The Cairngorm feeling of this country is mainly due to the strewn blocks and the granite escarpments of the central spine stretching from Craiglee over Craignaw to Mullwharchar and the Tauchers forming the highest cliffs above strings of lochs. The pale biotitic granite has resisted erosion, but the lochs occupy depressions where it has been under chemical attack.

To appreciate it fully you must take a look at the lochs of the Doon Basin, which should include Loch Enoch, the remotest and the finest of all the hill lochs yet not much further to walk than a mile beyond Loch Arron. Here is a very special place indeed, a strange ragged loch with islands at 1,617 ft ringed by naked rock slabs and strewn with boulders as if the ice had melted yesterday. And above it on the west, the Merrick, 2,770 ft, highest peak in Galloway, able to withstand denudation because, when the molten granite was intruded in the adjacent cauldron, its sedimentary rocks were metamorphosed by the heat into harder material, as happened too on Corserine, its near rival in height.

So Loch Enoch, like the Dungeon lochs over the hills below Corserine, is on a boundary of rock types, though it is by far the most uneven loch in Galloway, like a ragged butterfly pinned on a mount of granite, flecked with black spots which are islands. The biggest island has its own loch on it. Mr J McBain in his informative book, *The Merrick and the Neighbouring Hills* tells the crafty story of how he chiselled through the ice in March 1918 to measure Loch Enoch for depth, since the absence of a boat had prevented any surveyors from doing so.

overleaf: Glen Trool

He proved it to be the deepest loch in South Scotland at the time, 20–30 ft deeper than Loch Doon before the hydro-electric alterations deepened the latter loch. McBain was able to cross the deep water on the ice to the big island, and in that lower wing of the butterfly was able to get soundings of 63, 85, 96, 127, 105 and 57 ft, while in the opposite wing to the south-east he got 50, 56 and 64 ft on a loch not quite covered over with ice, so he was a brave man working all alone up there. That night he stayed with the shepherd at Backhill of Bush in the Dee Valley, tramping the 17 miles to Dalmellington next day.

Great changes have come on this land since he wrote his book published in 1929. The shepherd has long since gone from Backhill of Bush and vast plantations of commercial trees have spread up the loneliest lanes, 'lane' meaning a stream in Galloway, though the term is meant to denote one connecting two lochs. The outlet from Loch Enoch to Loch Doon is by the Eglin Lane in which was caught a 4 lb Loch Enoch trout a long time ago.

These trout described by McBain, though not from personal knowledge, are said to have had no lower half to the tail, nor complete ventral fins, and he speculates that the adaptation may be due to the rock and sharp sandy bottom of this rock basin. It certainly seems strange that they should now be extinct if they managed to live long enough in this high loch to adapt.

Anyone visiting Loch Enoch should walk over the naked rock slabs and look at the strewn rocks of the icefall left by the shrinking Merrick glacier. Better still go on and climb nearby Mullwharchar, the highest of the pure granite peaks situated in the centre of the aureole of metamorphism. From here you have Merrick to the west and Corserine to the east and the cauldron lochs at your feet, with the crags of The Tauchers falling into Gala Lane. Here indeed is a Cairngorm feeling, intensified if you walk the ridge to Craignaw and drop to Cornarroch Strand, itself a miniature Lairig Ghru.

Under the Fang of the Merrick lies tiny Loch Twachtan, one of a dozen lochs draining into Loch Doon. This circular little loch swarms with tiny fish which are said to have large heads in proportion to

Loch Arron beneath the Merrick

Loch Enoch, the most remote of the Galloway rock basins

The head of Loch Doon

their size – perhaps another effect of extreme isolation. This smallest loch and the largest, Loch Macaterick, drain into Eglin Lane, the latter covering half a square mile with the large Blaeberry Island. Macaterick receives the outflow from Loch Fanny at its north end, and both contain trout.

From here we enter the field of domestic water supply and hydro-electricity developments, with Loch Doon sending its water by tunnel to power 4 generating stations *en route* to the Solway, while some of its catchment goes the other way to Ayr from Lochs Finlas, Derclach, Riecawr, Goosie, Ballochling and Gower. The only loch feeding Loch Doon from the east side is Loch Muck on the Dalmellington–Carspharin road where the Water of Deugh is harnessed to feed Loch Doon.

The raising of Loch Doon by the building of dams at the north and north-eastern ends gives it a possible variation in level of 40 ft. In pre-reservoir days its measurements were as follows: length 6 miles, maximum breadth $1\frac{1}{2}$ miles, mean breadth $\frac{1}{3}$ of a mile, maximum depth 100 ft, mean depth 27 ft. The main visual difference today is that the loch has a greater superficial area giving it more width and dignity. The salmon and brown trout fishing from the banks is free and boats can be hired.

Geologically the loch is of special interest, since the aureole of metamorphism passes through it, so that one basin is granite – the deep one nearest to the high hills – while the north basin is in softer Silurian strata. The famous fourteenth century castle, removed from its island and rebuilt on the shore, overlooks the granite area. Its stones were relaid in the original manner and show the unusual shape with 11 unequal sides 26 ft high and over 7 ft thick. The entrance is by a fine pointed doorway. The island on which it stood may always have been a place of refuge for early man judging by a find of nine tree-trunk canoes on the loch bottom close to it.

The water of Loch Doon released eastward by outlet valve is used 4 times through a chain of 4 power stations before discharging into the Solway at Kirkcudbright. Built between 1931 and 1936 it has long since repaid the £3m. spent on it and was the only big development of those days of depression. It took maximum advantage of catchment in this southern hill country, establishing a completely new

The hill country of Loch Doon

Loch Doon

loch at Clatteringshaws as a second reservoir, with a third in Loch Ken, giving $\frac{1}{3}$ storage against $\frac{2}{3}$ river to produce 226 million units annually.

Once the water has been released from Loch Doon through the valve in Cairsphairn Lane it goes through the headponds of Kendoon Loch, Carsfad Loch, Earlston Loch and Loch Ken to Tongland. Clatteringshaws is broadly triangular and lies to the west of the Ken Valley, the water being led by $3\frac{1}{2}$ miles of tunnel to Glenlee power station before joining the Ken. Good places to stay are the villages of St John's Town of Dalry and New Galloway, two of the most architecturally delightful in Galloway, superbly situated in gentle farming country and looking out on river and hills. Fishing permits for lochs and rivers can be had at Milton Park Hotel, Dalry, and Cross Keys Hotel, New Galloway, or from the Dalry Angling Association for Carsfad and Clatteringshaws, at 20p and 50p per day respectively. The salmon and sea trout fishing in Loch Ken is free to hotel guests.

Loch Ken belongs to the Dee drainage system, which by hydro-electric engineering begins nowadays at Loch Doon as has been explained. To trace the original drainage we must go back into the heart of the hills and look at two Loch Dungeons. The remotest is the Round Loch of the Dungeon under Dungeon Hill. It lies close to the watershed of the Great Valley separating the granite of the Mullwharchar and the baked rocks of the Rhinns of Kells and contains trout and pike. Just below it is the Long Loch of the Dungeon, said to be infested with pike, and with maybe a salmon among the trout. The height difference between the lochs is only 30 ft, and the Long Loch trails into the sinister Silver Flow, the most dangerous raised bog in Galloway and one that has claimed at least one life.

It takes its name from the glitter of pools in the centre of the bog which is actively growing west of Cooran Lane though one part lies in the loop where the Cornarroch Strand joins the Lane. The Nature Conservancy has leased Silver Flow in order to study it, and one of the methods used has been to take low level aerial photographs of the pools with an auto-

overleaf 218/219 : Earlston Loch, a headpond of the Galloway power scheme

overleaf 220/221 : Winter at Clatteringshaws reservoir

matic camera suspended from a balloon. Sheep avoid the place and the largest dragonflies in Galloway buzz around the bladderwort in summer.

Loch Dee is a pleasant walk from the head of Loch Trool or from Clatteringshaws and contains trout, salmon, pike and eels. It is a true rock basin, broadest at the south-west end where it is deepest. Length just over a mile with a maximum breadth of $\frac{3}{4}$ of a mile, more than half the loch is covered by less than 10 ft, the maximum being 36 ft west of the big peninsula which nearly divides the loch into two. Fishing can be arranged with the Cross Keys Hotel, New Galloway.

Another Loch Dungeon is in the Rhinns of Kells, approached from above Earlston Loch from Polharrow Bridge by one of the most delightful glens in Galloway. The road ends at Forrest Lodge beyond which it is a walk of 3 miles or so into the hills, through forestry plantations at first. Nestling under the steep screes of Milldown and Millyea it has great character, 1,000 ft up and nearly a mile long by $\frac{1}{3}$ of a mile maximum breadth, a big peninsula almost dividing its irregular shape. As might be expected the rock basin is deepest under the peaks, reaching 94 ft, shallowing to 34 ft in the centre and deepening again to 45 ft. Two smaller of the Dee lochs lying northward are Loch Minnoch and Loch Harrow, the latter a rock basin with a maximum depth of 29 ft. The fishing appears to be private.

Loch Grannoch takes us back to the granite again under Cairnsmore of Fleet in the Cairn Edward Forest, a narrow rock basin 2 miles long by over $\frac{1}{3}$ of a mile broad with a maximum depth of 68 ft. Brown trout fishing at 40p per day can be arranged with Cally Estate Office, Gatehouse-of-fleet, also from Cally Hotel in the same country town.

Loch Skerrow lies further east and the brown trout fishing is 50p per day from Cally Estate Office as above. This loch is $\frac{3}{4}$ of a mile long by $\frac{1}{2}$ a mile in maximum breadth with a greatest depth of 33 ft, though 40 per cent is less than 10 ft deep. All this is noted wild goose country, attracting ornithologists from autumn to spring when pink feet, greylags, barnacle, Greenland whitefronts and even the rare lesser whitefronts may be encountered.

Woodhall Loch lies below New Galloway on the Laurieston road and is $1\frac{3}{4}$ miles long by nearly $\frac{1}{3}$ of a

Granite Dungeon Hill throws an abrupt shoulder to the Dry Loch

Loch Ken, the finest wildlife loch in Galloway

mile broad, partly a rock basin with a maximum
depth of 49 ft. And now we come to Loch Ken,
greatly elongated to make a reservoir for the Galloway
Power Scheme but still the finest wildlife loch in the
neighbourhood thanks to the diversity of its shores and
rich feeding for birds. Loch Ken contains enough
water to run the Tongland Power Station for 24 hours
at full load, controlled by barrage gates at its southern
end. Yet it does not look like a reservoir.

In pre-hydro-electric days Loch Ken was just over
$4\frac{1}{2}$ miles long with a maximum width of $\frac{1}{2}$ a mile and
a maximum depth of 62 ft near the top end in the
deepest of 6 rock basins. And beneath where the loch
ended there were expansions of the Dee, one of them
nearly $\frac{1}{2}$ a mile in width, with depths of 44 ft and 42 ft,
in parts separated by a mile of winding. The barrage
and added inflow from the north has made a 10-mile
loch of all this, narrowest near Parton where the
disused railway crosses by bridge. There is no monotony

in any stretch of this loch, with its farmlands and forests and grassy hillocks often thronged with cropping grey geese and sleeping wigeon duck. Glass the loch and you will find pintail, teal, shoveller, mallard, golden eye and many another in the bays or out on the narrow loch. Over the hills you may see buzzards or spot a peregrine falcon. Man has super-imposed himself graciously here, even to architectur-ally satisfying villages like Parton and Crossmichael. Just a few miles on is shallow Carlingwark Loch at Castle Douglas, 17 ft at its deepest and popular for fishing and boating. The extensive National Trust for Scotland gardens at Threave nearby should be visited for its views and parklands as much as for its wealth of exotic flowers. Part of the estate is a wildfowl reserve.

Before leaving Galloway a mention must be made of the connected lochs of the Girvan basin which begin just north of the Merrick on the hill called Shalloch on Minnoch with Loch Girvan's Eye nearly 1,500 ft up, a tiny sheet of water full of trout and relatively accessible from the high-climbing Straiton road in a walk of less than 3 miles. In the connected staircase of lochs below, the next is Loch Cornish $1\frac{1}{2}$ miles distant and three times as big, though the length is only $\frac{1}{4}$ of a mile by $\frac{1}{7}$ of a mile broad, with a maximum depth of 7 ft. Below it in another $1\frac{1}{2}$ miles is Loch Skelloch about the same size and holding good trout.

Another $1\frac{1}{2}$ miles down is Loch Lure and Loch Bradan, now joined together to make a reservoir to supply domestic water to Troon. Bradan fed by Loch Brecbowie was originally a few feet lower in elevation than Lure. Joining them together has not submerged completely the ruins of a building on the island purported to be a castle. The original depth of Lure and Bradan was 7 ft maximum and 8 ft maximum respectively. Raised by 10 ft they make one loch of just under 2 miles connected by road to Tairlaw. Fishing permits cost 25p per day, and boats 50p. They may be had from the Forestry Commission, Craigard, Straiton, Maybole.

Galloway is in the process of change and there are two extreme views about the huge-scale forestry operations which are crowding up valley after valley in a dark green tide of spruces. The forester says you cannot have too many trees, and points out the 205 sq. miles of Glen Trool Forest Park, which was a region in

decline when the Commission took over. Until then the vast areas of hill land had been divided into sheep farms. There are five productive forests now, yet the country of Kirkcudbright as a whole still carries the same population of sheep. Grazings have been much improved, say the Forestry Commission, due to the use of lime and fertilisers to reseed the fire-breaks which are let out to local sheep men. The network of forestry roads have also been of use to the farmers by reducing their isolation.

In human terms there is a new village of 47 houses with shop and school in Glen Trool. Eighteen small-holdings have been let to forest workers. The population has gone up here but has decreased elsewhere in Kirkcudbright. On the recreation side there has been a steadily increasing use with something like 25,000 caravanners and campers using the Glen Trool site annually so that the whole area is being enjoyed as never before in its history.

Against this, however, is the view of the shepherd and the naturalist. The first would say that the plant-ings are going too far and that there will soon be no

Carlingwark Loch, Castle Douglas

Glen Trool forestry village

Farming and forestry combine below Cairnsmore of Fleet

room left for his sheep. They plead that the time has come when positive conservation is required to save the farms and preserve the habitats before they disappear under trees, diminishing the wide views of moors and sky which are such an inspiring feature of Galloway. It is said now that there is two acres of productive forest for each of the 58,000 inhabitants in the two counties of Wigtown and Kirkcudbright. Forestry is expected to provide for 4,000 people in Galloway eventually, including workers and their families.

Perhaps what is needed in Galloway is something akin to the Cairngorm Nature Reserve to conserve the maximum variety of some of the best bits of Galloway so that the wildlife continues to be rich. The area I would like to see covered by some form of agreement would be the piece to the west and east of Cairnsmore of Fleet, to protect the farms and the habitats before they are all taken over, since even in Galloway good planting land is getting scarce.

Lochs of the Annan Basin

Loch Skeen, Mill Loch, Kirk Loch, Castle Loch and Hightae Loch

Loch Skeen is a rarity for the Southern Uplands, a corrie loch 1,750 ft high between 2,600-ft hills. Moreover, in the Grey Mare's Tail dropping 200 ft into space it has the finest waterfall outside the Highlands. Add to that rare flowers, wild goats, a glacial tangle of moraines and you have a place of exceptional interest, especially with St Mary's loch lying only a short distance to the north-east.

Ponded by moraines, elongated Loch Skeen is $\frac{3}{4}$ of a mile long by only $\frac{1}{5}$ of a mile broad, with a centrally placed maximum depth of 36 ft and a mean of 18 ft. The best way to it is by the path known as Fraser's Brae which traverses the hill about 2 miles west of the Grey Mare's Tail. It is also practicable to take the National Trust path up the east side of the Tail Burn, enjoy the sight of the foaming waterfall, and carry on beyond, picking your way as best you can. Warning notices telling you to beware of the steep ground below the path should be carefully regarded, as deaths have occurred here from slipping into the ravine. There is a shorter way of seeing the waterfall by taking the west side of the Tail Burn, and it is all the more impressive for the viewpoint being low down since you get the full roar and spouting vigour of the fall.

The remaining lochs are grouped round Lochmaben near Lockerbie, a trim Royal Burgh with a proud statue of Robert Bruce who built his castle here, and the local tradition is that the hero was born in Lochmaben. The Castle Loch has the ruins of the Bruce stronghold on a wooded promontory, all that is left of a much besieged place. The loch itself is the largest in the basin and is a fine example of a eutrophic (mineral rich) lowland loch said to contain pike, perch, roach, bream, chub and trout, though its vendace is now extinct, killed off by pollution apparently. It is a local nature reserve now, with Hightae Loch. The accent is on conserving the plants and wildlife, especially the large numbers of wildfowl which winter here. Castle Loch statistics are: length just over $\frac{3}{4}$ of a mile, maximum breadth $\frac{2}{3}$ of a mile, maximum depth 18 ft in the central part. The mean depth is $8\frac{1}{2}$ ft.

Wild goats of Loch Skeen

The Mill Loch still has vendace in it, the only loch in Scotland where *Coregonus vandesius* occurs, a 6- to 8-in. fish which spawns in November and December. Brown-backed, sides tinged with yellow, it has a heart-shaped mark between the eyes. There is a tradition that they were introduced here by Queen Mary, no doubt as a tasty dish, for they were once netted in fair numbers, and there was even a club devoted to catching enough for an annual banquet. Situated immediately north of Lochmaben the length is ½ a mile by ⅕ of a mile with a maximum depth of 55 ft at the southern end. It is a kettle-hole in fluvio-glacial gravels.

Kirk Loch is edged by a modern housing development now, in good taste to match the quality of the view from their windows. The length is just under ½ a mile by ⅕ of a mile, the maximum depth being

25 ft though over half is covered by less than 10 ft of water.

Hightae Loch is shaped like a narrow upside-down pear, only ⅓ of a mile at its broadest where the water is deepest at 13 ft, with an overall mean of 7 ft. Hightae Loch takes its name from the Royal Town to the south called Hightae, just a hamlet like Greenhill, Smallholm and Heck which are the other three 'Royal Towns' of Lochmaben. Much of the troubled history of the Scottish border was made here at this western frontier with England. Even in 1628 fines imposed upon cattle drovers were allocated to the upkeep of the King's castle at Lochmaben. A lot of money would be taken this way, for the cattle trade to England was considerable. In 1663 something like 18½ thousand beasts passed through the Carlisle toll gate. How many slipped across the border without paying will never be known.

overleaf: Lochmaben, dinghy sailing

Lochs of the Tweed Basin
St Mary's Loch, Loch of the Lowes and Talla Reservoir

Anyone with an eye for country travelling north-eastwards along Moffatdale will notice the deep ' U ' shape of the valley, its straightness the result of glaciation along the shatter belt, the same influence that gives us the Grey Mare's Tail, most conspicuous of several hanging tributaries above the road leading to St Mary's and Loch of the Lowes – two separate lochs which used to be one. The barrier between the lochs at Tibbie Shiels Inn which carries the road is no more than debris pushed out by the Ox Cleuch Burn to the west and the Thirlstane Burn to the east meeting together to form a natural dam.

Even St Mary's Loch as it is today is divided into two basins by a big fan of alluvium built up by the Megget Water where it enters half way down the loch. Similarly the loch level has been raised by the deltas which pond its outlet. The dam in this case has been built up by the Kirkstead and Dryhope Burns to the north, and the Thorny Cleuch to the south. The glacier which dug the trench containing St Mary's Loch spilled over from Moffatdale and Megget to make a rock basin continuing its digging action into Yarrow to leave a mass of morainic litter.

In this country of fine glens and rounded hills with its few lochs, two great native writers, Sir Walter Scott and James Hogg, drew inspiration here for their novels. They would often meet together to carouse at Tibbie Shiels, and delight in each other's opposites, Scott the man of infinite culture, Hogg the self-taught Ettrick shepherd and poet who wrote the amazing *Confessions of a Justified Sinner* now regarded as a classic. It is a psychological horror story, haunting in its conviction of evil turned on its perpetrator to madness and suicide. Nothing like it had been written before, or since.

Hogg's seated statue in bronze, with his '. . . auld, towzy, trusty dog' Hector, looks over the Loch of the Lowes outside Tibbie Shiels Inn, as if reflecting on all the big trout he caught. Permits are available at 38p and £1 for a boat on both lochs by applying to the Gordon Arms Hotel, the Rondono Hotel, the Glen Café or The Old Schoolhouse, Cappercleuch. Large parties must make special arrangements with St Mary's Angling Club, 4 Gladstone Terrace, Edinburgh 9, telephone 667 4851.

Loch of the Lowes is a mile long by $\frac{1}{4}$ of a mile broad with a maximum depth of 58 ft at the southern end. St Mary's is just under 3 miles with a maximum breadth of over $\frac{1}{2}$ a mile and a maximum depth of 153 ft in its widest part where the Megget glacier joined the Moffat glacier. This shallows to 88 ft where the ridge of gravel brought down by the Megget has built up a ridge, beyond which is the southern basin which drops to 112 ft and continues deeply for $\frac{1}{2}$ a mile.

St Mary's Loch with its ruins of the old chapel and Dryhope Tower is a popular motor run today, but it does not yield its full charms by this flighty mode of travel. To catch the spirit of the place you should leave the car at Tibbie Shiels and take a walk along the foot-path following along by the March Wood to the farm of Bowerhope. South of the Gordon Arms Hotel above the Yarrow is a farmhouse called Eldinhope. James Hogg who died in 1835 lived there. A memorial service to persecuted Covenanters who died for their faith is held every year in the ruins of St Mary's Chapel.

A narrow road running from Cappercleuch climbs through the hills to Talla Reservoir and drops by waterfalls into the deep glacial gouge now occupied by a long narrow loch impounded behind 1,300 ft of embankment to supply Edinburgh with water. The natural drainage is into the Tweed. Begun in 1895 the work was finished in 1905, and the brown trout fishing is in the hands of the Corporation Water Department, 6 Cockburn Street, Edinburgh, 30p per boat and 20p per rod.

Talla Reservoir is 959 ft above sea-level and 14 miles south of Peebles in Tweedale. Length $2\frac{1}{2}$ miles by $\frac{1}{4}$ of a mile broad, the maximum depth of 73 ft is near the embankment. It is an easy matter to climb the highest hill in the Southern Uplands from Talla, Broad Law, 2,754 ft, by striking north from the Megget Stane on the highest point of the road above the Talla Linns.

The lines to the Galloway novelist S R Crockett written by Robert Louis Stevenson sum up the feeling of this rolling country of secret glens:

Grey recumbent tombs of the dead in desert places,
Standing-stones on the vacant wine-red moor,
Hills of sheep, and the howes of the silent vanished races,
And winds, austere and pure . . .

Selected Bibliography

Ancient monuments of Scotland V G Childe and W D Simpson, HMSO 1961

The Shetland Isles A T Clunes, Robert Hale 1956

The companion guide to the West Highlands of Scotland W H Murray, Collins 1968

Game Fishing in Inverness-shire
Game Fishing in Shetlands
Game Fishing in Orkney } J Coutts
Game Fishing in Outer Hebrides
Game Fishing in Mainland Ross & Cromarty W Brown, Highland Development Board booklets

West Highland survey Fraser F Darling, Oxford University Press 1955

Highways and Byways in West Highlands Seton Gordon, Macmillan 1935

The drove roads of Scotland A R B Haldane, Edinburgh University Press 1968

A hundred years in the Highlands O Mackenzie, Bles 1965

Scottish Historical Review vol. xlix, 1, no. 147, 'The Scottish "Iron Age"' Euan W MacKie, April 1970

A description of the Western Isles of Scotland Martin Martin (1703) reprint James Thin (1970)

The Merrick and neighbouring hills J M McBain, Stephen and Pollock

Galloway: the spell of its hills and glens Andrew McCormick, John Smith 1947

The Hebrides W H Murray, Heinemann 1966

British regional geology—Scotland: The northern Highlands J Phemister, HMSO 1968

Index